HOW TO
WIN
YOUR
WORST
BATTLE

DIONNY & YARISSETTE BÁEZ

HOW TO
WIN
YOUR
WORST
BATTLE

www.DionnyBaez.com
ISBN: 978-0692-4072-9-5

Publishing director
Fabián Díaz Atencio
Design, layout
Luis Felipe Díaz
Cover page

Grammar, spelling and style review:
Yesmina Morales
José Eduardo Correror

Impreso en Colombia-Printed in Colombia
2016

DEDICATION

For the millionaire, the poor, the powerful and the weak. For the seven billion people who must inevitably wage battles in so many areas of their lives, in so many parts of the world, I hope through these pages they can discover the victorious individuals they carry within.

For our children, Shaddai, Salome and those to come. You are the climax of our victories.

For you Lord, your fidelity has left us speechless.

CONTENTS

Book One

Dionny

INTRODUCTION

"At this point in my life I had a considerable list of near-death experiences, including very critical and difficult situations, but nothing was as painful and exhausting until what happened next.

Each battle carries within itself its own victory, and each process brings learning. The impressive journey you are about to embark on through these pages will be no exception.

Through my experiences, some advice I have applied, but above all, through the many errors involved in the process, I have acquired some principles that I know will help you to not only win, but also understand the reason for your battle. These principles will be discussed through each chapter.

The Principle of
BALANCE

1

I Starting a book like this is not an easy task. For example: which of the impressive events from recent years should I use to start this fascinating story?

Maybe I can start by telling you about the character who appeared supernaturally in my room that morning to communicate the message that started everything... no. It could be the revelation I received immediately after 41 days of fasting... or perhaps with the accurate prophecy given by Paul Lay, the Patagonia prophet who predicted in detail everything that would happen, two years before it happened... well, every event will come in its time, but why not start with that cold day in January of two thousand and ten...

After what seemed like three endless years of countless legal trials, long days and over-whelming challenges, at last, everything would be defined today. Every year that had passed I had to face the shame of feeling naked before so many spectators, but today, today everything was about to change, or at least that was what I believed.

It was the final court date, the long-awaited day, when my future would be decided, an uncertain future when I considered that if I was found guilty, I might lose my freedom for a while, or worse, lose my legal status in the country forever which, although it was not my birth country, I had worked for so long to build a future and a purpose here. If so, all my years of work would be ineffective and I would find myself again in Venezuela, my native country, and would have to start from scratch.

I looked at the clock, it was 9:13 in the morning, surely my heart was beating much faster than the seconds of that clock. Although I clung to my faith, I cannot deny that I was sweating, not only because I still wore my coat that cold winter, but because I feared that anything could happen, even the things that terrified me at the time.

We arrived at room 1103 of the court of Philadelphia. Just before opening the majestic red wooden door I felt my right hand being squeezed. It was Yarissette, my brave wife, who through all these years had fought with me in this arduous battle. Behind her was her mother and her two sisters. Besides them, my mother, how could she not attend? She knew the truth from behind the curtain, and she marched like an army after a sure victory.

We were sure we would win our case, but what if the opposite happened? What to do when you are so sure that if you have the truth you will win every battle, but things do not go as you expected?

Often, as human beings, we must fight many battles. Some are family battles, others are physical, -such as diseases and limitations- others are spiritual, and emotional. We often do not understand the reason.

Balance and the butterfly

"Every time you blink, the stars move".

Emerson.

Edward Lorenz started it all four decades ago. As a meteorological researcher at MIT he created a computer program designed to model the climate. Lorenz had reduced climate change to a series of formulas that behaved in recognizable weather patterns.

In his book on Chaos, James Gleick recounts the winter day in 1961 when, after having to make a climactic impression, Lorenz wanted to save time by starting from the middle. To give the machine the initial condition, he wrote the same numbers as the last climatic impression.

Something unexpected happened. He noticed that his new mock climate pattern diverged dramatically from his past impression.

First, he thought the computer had malfunctioned. Suddenly, he understood. This was not a machine error. The answer was in the numbers he had inserted into the computer. In the original programming, he had used six decimal places: .506127. The second time he simplified the numbers to .506. He assumed that the difference -a portion of a thousand- would have no impact. He was wrong. This made a BIG difference. Introducing this small change produced a huge result!

The formal name of this phenomenon is "sensitive dependence under initial conditions". Its informal and much more popular name is "The butterfly effect".

Presented in a simpler way, it means that the tiny changes that a butterfly can produce by moving its wings in San Francisco, have the power to transform the climatic condition in Shanghai.

Countless times we feel like butterflies before the torrential giants of life and we feel helpless, incapable of transforming the situation. This could explain perfectly how I felt that day, not knowing yet that the tiny flapping of a butterfly could create a tornado on the other side of the world.

As we opened the doors of that Court, the faint shriek of wood against wood, which elsewhere would have gone unnoticed, interrupted the sepulchral silence that was there. Immediately, the faces of those who were already seated turned around. For my peace of mind no one knew me, or at least no one seemed to know me. They were other possibly guilty people, who like me, would have to face the judge to prove otherwise.

— *"Let's sit down at the front,* —said Yarissette said in a nervous but firm voice—. *I want the Judge to see us until it is our turn.*

Although she did not say so, I know that Yarissette expected the judge to perceive our spirit. Shortly after Jamie entered, a young lawyer whom we met by chance (which I will recount later) and had hired to represent us.

—*Do not worry* — Jamie said after greeting us—. *We have already won the first part of the case and I am quite sure that we will win in the end today,* — he added with the little Spanish that he spoke.
— *What's the plan?* —I asked—. *You will wait here until our turn comes, then I will do everything, you will not say anything unless it is necessary,* — he replied with a half-smile.

—*Please stand*— a loud voice in English broke off—. *Honorable Judge Harold Kane,* — the voice continued as the private door opened and the Judge entered. The same judge who we had tried to summon for three years to end this case, which, although was of little importance to the system (compared to the complicated cases under his responsibility), for us represented the most important one of our lives.

As the trials began to unfold before us, I was still aware of how vulnerable we seemed before the system. It was there, at that very moment, that things began to seem clearer to me.

—*Where is the victory really? What is it about being a winner, being victorious?*

I went back to the Bible stories my parents told me as a child. Samson against the Philistines. Young Gideon with his army of three hundred men inspiring Hollywood to produce the film titled after that number. The great difference between Sparta and Gideon was that in the end he not only won, but came out alive. David and Goliath, Moses and Pharaoh, conflicts of a great number of real characters that in the end were colossal victories, which are mentioned until today.

I concluded that they should all have principles in common.

Principles are a set of simple, yet powerful, models to help us understand how the world works. These principles generate the same result all the time, no matter where, when, or who uses them. Principles work when you apply them.

Gravity is a principle. When you get up you do not question yourself about where your feet will go when you get out of bed. They go down, never up. In the same way two plus two equals four. It will never be equal to five. Principles never wear out, never get tired, and never disappear. Principles cannot be overused. Life is the process of discovering principles.

When I remembered the characters in the fascinating stories they told me as a child, I realized that what I was going through was nothing compared to their circumstances, and that if I discovered those principles and applied them to my life, I would also be a winner.

I will call these historical characters "victorious individuals". Today I realize that the first universal principle of victorious individuals is "balance".

Adversity is the force of balance

Your peace will be equivalent to the measure of comfort you can have with paradox, contradiction, confusion and ambiguity.

How I would have liked at that moment to know the power of balance as I know it now!

At the time, I did not see it, but as time passed I would realize that victory depends on the balance I am able to achieve between what I am going through and the benefit that my situation will eventually bring to my life.

Balance is the interaction between being, feeling, thinking and doing. Those winners from Sacred History integrated these four foundations of existence into the turbulence of the world and daily activity, and in so doing, could creatively solve any challenge they faced and thus, created an atmosphere of empowerment and love wherever they were.

The story of these victorious individuals is ours. These stories become metaphors for the challenges and conflicts we face in our own lives, and the power we must find to overcome the challenges and continually evolve.

David's classic challenge against the giant is the very one we must deal with, against our very existence. The afflictions he faced are manifested as emotional conflicts with those we love and work, injustices, consequences, spiritual and ethnic dilemmas that ignite the collision between reason and spirituality in the constant evolution of the problems that surround us. All of us are subject to this torrent of changes.

In that moment, I was still struggling to understand why I had to go through what I was going through.

Many of us are tirelessly trying to find meaning within a rigid and static understanding of the world as I did. It is very easy to fall into the melodrama of being a victim, trying to find the why of all things, especially those that we do not believe deserve our good conduct or integrity. Then I realized that in order to have the right balance, you have to have the correct answers, to have the correct answers, you have to ask the right questions, and the correct question is not why? But rather: what for?

What do you gain by finally understanding the "why"? The answer to that question will always be based on the past; and the past is something that we cannot change. While "what for?" is grounded in the future and gives you the clarity to make relevant decisions in the present, because your future will never be better than the decisions you can make today.

It is possible that your battle has a greater purpose than life itself.

From this perspective, it is possible to find balance, and balance is the only place to begin.

According to Friedrich Nietzsche, "astronomy (the science that studies the planets) has discovered that only chaos can give birth to a star". This is what victorious individuals do. They connect with their own existence and reconcile the pulling and pushing of life.

Victorious individuals are strengthened when there is confusion and chaos because no matter how much insanity may come up, they remain entrenched. They instinctively understand that life is a confluence of meanings, relationships and contexts. Victorious individuals recognize that, to find harmony, we must balance all the forces that surround us. In short words, the victors balance the forces of despair and tranquility, good and evil, anger and serenity within themselves and from there forge an identity that is powerful and purposeful. One of the most renowned prophets of the Old Testament was the prophet Elijah, who at the time of his greatest despair sought to hear the Voice of God. Suddenly an earthquake came, it was logical to think (based on the feeling he felt) that God would speak to him through the earthquake, which was equivalent to his despair, but God was not there. A tempestuous fire came and God was not there either. But, paradoxically, it was in the gentle whisper of the wind that he found His Voice.

Balance is achieved by recognizing all the opposing forces in the universe and having the ability to take advantage of them.

The cosmos itself is a collection of all these forces that have existed since the creation of time and space. Light and darkness, good times and bad times, ups and downs, and any other setbacks that saturate our universe. These setbacks are what give life to our action. It is the flow and even the collision of these forces that generate life itself.

The history of human civilization is just another example of this. For a Martin Luther King Jr., it took racism, for a Ghandi a Hitler was needed and thanks to a Judas we have a Glorified Christ.

Ego unbalances us, conflict defines us

— *We have lived long enough to write several books*
— Yarissette whispered to my ear, referring to the

many experiences lived in spite of our young age, hers, twenty-four and mine, twenty-nine.

Time passed as we looked at the clock, every second seemed like hours and the hours, days, while we waited impatiently for our turn. I did not know that when the time came, a series of unexpected events would be unleashed.

Superficially it did not seem like a big problem, but to me it was, or maybe I should say, for my ego.

At the age of eight I began to preach. At the age of seventeen, after graduating high school, I devoted myself full time to evangelism. At the age of nineteen I experienced forty-one days of fasting, in which I received a deep spiritual revelation which launched me onto international platforms. After writing books, conducting mass conferences and producing television programs in more than seventy countries, I had created a certain expectation for many people. An image that undoubtedly hung in the balance, especially when confronted with the idea that many people had of this trial. An international show program had propagated a totally different story to what the trial was about. I think it was the factor that caused me more pain, since I knew that if I did not win the trial I would not only lose my freedom with the possibility of being deported, but this distorted story would spread more strongly, destroying me forever. How wrong I was with this endless struggle to protect my image. Today I understand that my worst enemy was not the prosecutor, the Judge, or those who attacked me. My worst enemy would lead me into making the worst decisions. My worst enemy was my ego.

From this state of being, you live in imbalance. It is the ego that causes you to be overwhelmed by a combination of feelings that incapacitate your best ability to make decisions: anger, disappointment, euphoria, sadness. All these emotions talk to you at the same time, which one of them should you embrace? Which of these emotions are positive, which are negative? How do you react correctly amid the most critical situation in a battle?

A victorious individual has realized that the negative side of emotions is not the emotions themselves, but the approach you take with them. Fighting from the ego makes us unbalanced, since it makes us believe that all history, including our own, is defined by absolute good, that what produces anger, sadness or disappointment is always negative. This is not true, since anything that lacks contrast - the friction between good and evil - becomes banal and inert. Jesus himself had to face His Gethsemane.

We ourselves are the amalgam of these emotions.

Have you ever felt so consumed by anger or frustration that you wanted to go through the wall with a fist or throw the remote control out of the window? Then you have felt the force that drove Moses to continue in the desert or what motivated Paul to not surrender.

Have you ever felt the need to avenge the wrong that another person has caused? It is the same need that inspired Esther to free her people from a certain death.

If these are known emotions, then you already know what defines a winner. Now, how can we consciously maintain balance at critical moments? How can we undertake intelligent attitudes instead of reacting from the ego to the torrent of emotions and demands around us? How can we find peace in our daily lives and make that peace resonate through our actions?

The principle of the answer is: keeping sobriety.

In this case sobriety means: being centered and maintaining total focus. The same approach that Jesus had to look beyond the Cross. Staying sober allows a person to make focused and effective decisions.

Winners do not surrender to anything that limits the quality of their focus. On the contrary, staying sober, emotionally fresh and energetic allows them to exist in a state of expanded focus, in which no amount of discomfort or battles takes away the peace for any amount of time.

True experiences of joy, peace, and love can only be found from a state of total focus. These experiences come from being connected to the spirit.

The characteristics of the spirit are those of nature itself.

The natural responses of the universe are to be in balance, be it with the environment, the seasons, or even the metabolism of our own bodies. When something goes out of balance, nature spontaneously seeks to restore balance. The only thing that can stop this restoration process is when we limit it by introducing some artificial toxicity to the system.

Sobriety governs the ego

"The wind blows where it wishes, and you hear the sound of it, but cannot tell where it comes from and where it goes. So is everyone who is born of the Spirit..."

(John 3:8 NKJV).

Winners maintain sobriety because they produce emotional well-being. Emotional well-being is sustained by freeing ourselves from emotional poisons, such as hostility, resentment, fear, guilt, and depression. Let us better understand these:

- Hostility: this is remembering the pain and the desire to pay with retribution.
- Fear: this is the anticipation of pain.
- Guilt: this is self-inflicting pain when you blame yourself.
- Depression: this the depletion of energy as a result of the above.

I realized that victorious individuals are free from these toxic emotions, not by denying any emotional pain but by being in tune with it and surpassing it.

Because of their sobriety, true victors take responsibility for painful experiences without having to take the role of victims. The ability to express their experiences without blaming others, advancing and celebrating the freedom that comes from not clinging to the past frees them from becoming victims.

It is from this state of sobriety that you can apply the four main levels of existence: being, feeling, thinking and doing.

The first level of existence is BEING

Through the battles in my life, I realized that not living from being prolongs suffering and delays the processes of life. "Being" is the life that comes from the spirit. Those who are born of the spirit focus on the peace that comes from it. Our goal is to find the unshakeable tranquility that God has implanted within our being in the midst of the turbulence and chaos within the world around us.

The second level of existence is
FEELING

To feel is to be absolutely precise in our actions and not be distracted by the toxic impulses that weaken us, such as hatred, hostility, retribution, blindness and fears. It is not that there is empathy, but rather that there is a disciplined precision as to how conscious we are of our own feelings.

Being aware of what we feel ensures that each intention is the product of a balanced emotion. Feeling also means eliminating the need to be right and self-important. Victorious individuals never justify themselves.

The third level of existence is
THINKING

The highest form of thinking is creativity. It is to believe that there are no problems that cannot be solved by creativity. This way of thinking must be in line with the highest ideals of the spirit, which are: truth, benignity, harmony and patience, from which derive all the fruits of the spirit.

When decisions are deliberate and acted from this place of emotional centrality, the result will be transformative and positive.

The fourth and last level of existence is DOING

In many ways this is the culmination of the first three states of existence. It is to emerge from them by putting them into practice. This action must, of course, be in line with our being, feelings and thoughts, and the last four, with God, who is the one who reveals our spirit. Intuitively, when the moment of action comes, we will know what to do, and we will do it flawlessly, attracting in synchrony with those events that will make you win in the end, although in the present may seems like the opposite. My present at that moment seemed to go in my favor. While the prosecutor presented his argument, the symphony of the system began, a symphony that inevitably forces you to dance to its rhythm. The cavalry of modalities and suggestions in which the least fortunate individual is at risk.

But what else could happen? This trial depended on no hard evidence, but more on one person's word against another.

Jamie felt safe as the prosecutor continued. When he finished, Jamie did not hesitate to present his argument immediately. I could not believe that we had waited so many years for such a short trial.

—*"Your honor,"* our lawyer continued, *"the information the prosecutor has presented is totally wrong. My client has never been a pastor of a church, never separated from his wife, does not personally manage any social network, has never ...*
He took about fifteen minutes more refuting the last presentation of the prosecutor and concluded:
— *Therefore, my defendant must be exonerated.*

The judge requested a short recess before pronouncing his last word, since at his request, the trial did not have a jury. During the recess, young Jamie expressed his only concern:
— *I'm just afraid the judge wants to cut the baby.*
— *What do you mean?* — I replied.

He would then explain to me that this was a legal term referring to the biblical judgment in which king Solomon, undecided by the words of two different women claiming to be the legitimate mother of a baby, pretended to want to cut it in half to give it to both parties.

In fact, this trial was also divided in two parts, one that we had already won in 2008, and the pending one that was to be decided at that time.

—*All stand* — the voice repeated, indicating that the recess had ended and that the judge was making his entrance to end the trial.

Applying the principle of balance:

I will activate the principle of balance in my life by committing myself to take the next steps:

1. I will take a few minutes to pray today. I will meditate on the toxic relationships and situations to which I introduce myself, to gradually remove them from my life.

2. I will identify qualities in others that create resentment, frustration, stress, and hatred. I will recognize them and consider how to channel them into something more constructive.

3. Today I will acquire God's peace and focus on the positive of the worst of my situations.

The Principle
of
RESISTANCE

2

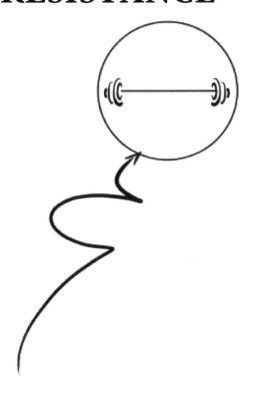

M oments like these I always remember ... The breeze in my hair, a sea as blue as the sky, the sand squeezing between my toes as they are occasionally rinsed by the foam of the waves. Everything seems perfect. After a strenuous tour, I had decided with Yarissette to take a day off to rest, not far from home. Atlantic City seemed like the ideal place for our spontaneous escapes. A city by the sea and only about forty-five minutes from Philadelphia.

It was a hot day at the end of June in 2007, three years before that final judgment. It would definitely be a day to remember, not only for the perfect time it had up until that moment, but for the unexpected call that would interrupt our rest. "A blocked number," I thought as I looked at my cell phone while deciding whether to answer it or not.

—*Is this Dionny Baez?* —A strange voice asked.

After answering, intrigued, I asked who was talking to me: —*William*— was his reply. He continued explaining to me that he was the creator of a blog on the internet that many read, which was responsible for disseminating information.

—I have things from you that I will divulge... unless we come to an arrangement, — the strange voice added.

At that moment, I was walking with my wife inside a small shopping mall that extended to the beach. Dumbfounded by the proposal and believing he was joking I activated my phone's loudspeaker so that Yarissette could hear it. You can imagine what our reaction was when we realized that the strange voice was serious. We hung up the phone that would be the start to a continuity of blocked calls during the next days and voice messages, which warned us that the attack had already begun.

I must admit that at first it seemed comical to us, especially when we read out of curiosity the scrawny stories that the individual wrote about us. We always preferred to be silent, until a call burst into silence. It was Moises Alicea, a friend worried about what he had just heard.

— Dionny, I was listening to the radio, I know what I heard and I am pretty sure they were talking about you.

— They would not dare do something like that — I said, referring to the Philadelphia radio station—, *but I will call them to make sure.*

Indeed, when I called, I realized that one of the announcers had read on the radio one of the stories that had been published so far. Although it seemed insignificant to me, I was indignant to know that someone would commit to do something like that.

—I only hear about this until now, but I promise you that I will talk to the announcer — said the radio station director via telephone and added— *Why don't you sue that William and close the blog?*
At that time, I made the first mistake you will ever make in your battle.

I was convinced that resistance was a counter-attack action. Then I realized that the greatest victorious individuals in history have won their battles not by paying wrong for evil. They have understood that resistance is not an external action but rather an internal condition. The most powerful resistance is to do nothing to achieve everything.

The book of Isaiah is a compilation of prophecies that were to occur during his time and in the times to come. Among them is the impressive prophecy about Jesus. The prophet Isaiah envisioned the terrible situation that the Messiah would have to face and gave the key to how he would win his worst battle:

> *"He was oppressed and He was afflicted, Yet He opened not His mouth; He was led as a lamb to the slaughter, and as a sheep before its shearers is silent, So He opened not His mouth".*

> **(Isaiah 53:7)**

Resistance for victorious individuals is a state of tranquility that keeps them calm. From that state of being, anything is possible.

Retaliation is not Resistance

"A complete human being knows without arriving, sees without seeing, and reaches everything without having done it".

The resistance of a victorious individual is the highest expression of his or her inner peace. This same concept of nature works without worrying about anything, with harmony and love. It does not try to be, it just is. When we learn this lesson from nature, we can easily achieve what we want.

When you observe nature in action, you realize this principle. Grass does not try to grow, it just grows, fish do not try to swim, they just do. Flowers do not try to be beautiful, they are. This is their intrinsic nature. The earth does not try to turn; it is its nature to turn at a high speed as it travels through space. It is the nature of a baby to be happy. The nature of the sun is to shine. The nature of the stars is to sparkle and shine. And the nature of a human being is to overcome every situation presented before an individual, easily and without concern. Jesus puts it this way: *"Therefore I say to you, do not worry about your life, what you will eat or what you will drink; nor about your body, what you will put on. Is not life more than food and the body more than clothing? Look at the birds of the air, for they neither sow nor reap nor gather into barns; yet your heavenly Father feeds them. Are you not of more value than they?... But seek first the kingdom of God and His righteousness, and all these things shall be added to you."*

The Kingdom of God is not a distant place in any part of our cosmic space, the Kingdom of God is a spiritual state where our happiness or tranquility does not depend on the point of view or our acceptance of another one but on an internal security. From this state of being, everything we resist will give up.

What we commonly call "miracles" is really the manifestation of the principle of resistance: doing less to achieve more. The resistance of a victorious individual is motivated by love, since the whole nature is maintained and developed by the force of love.

When you seek power and control over other people you lose strength. And you will need strength to win your battles. When you seek power to strengthen your ego, you lose strength by running behind the illusion of happiness, instead of enjoying the happiness of that moment. When you seek victories only by proving personal points, you cut off the flow of strength toward yourself and interfere with the wisdom of Creation. But when your actions are motivated by love there is no loss of strength. When your actions are motivated by "love", your forces multiply and accumulate.

Attention to the ego consumes the greatest amount of strength. When your reference point is your ego, when you seek control it over other people and their approval, you will lose your strength. But when your point of reference is the spirit, when you become immune to criticism and do not fear life's challenges, then you can reap the Power of Love, and use your strengths creatively to experience abundance and evolution.

Most of us strive to maintain our importance. If we could lose that importance a bit, two amazing things would happen to us. One, we would save strength by not trying to maintain the illusory idea of our greatness. Two, we would provide ourselves with sufficient strength to visualize a flash of God's Greatness.

Accept, be responsible, and do not defend yourself

"Every tormentor and tyrant is a mighty teacher".

There are three components that activate the principle of resistance within a winner.

1. The first one is ACCEPTANCE

Acceptance simply means making a decision: "Today I will accept people, circumstances and events as they are." It means that you will not fight against this moment because this moment is as it should be. Your acceptance of this moment is complete and total. You accept things as they are and not as you would wish them to be. It is very important that you understand this concept. You must have enough faith to believe that things are about to change and they will be different, but right now you must accept things as they are.

When you feel frustrated or angry about a person or situation, remember that you are not reacting to the person or situation, rather you are reacting to the expectations you have about that person or situation. These are your feelings and your feelings are not someone else's fault. When a winner recognizes and understands this completely, he or she takes responsibility for these situations and for all the events he or she sees as a problem.

2. This leads us to the second component of the principle of resistance: RESPONSIBILITY

What is responsibility? This means not focusing on someone's guilt, something or even of your own guilt, concerning this situation. While accepting a situation, event or battle, responsibility means the ability to have a creative response to the situation as it is now. A victorious individual understands that all battles contain a seed of victory, and this understanding leads them to take the moment and transform it into a better situation or thing.

When they do this, every supposedly frustrating situation becomes an opportunity for the creation of something new and beautiful. Reality is only a perception and if you choose to perceive reality in this way, you will have many opportunities to evolve.

3. The third component of the Resistance principle is "NO DEFENSE"

Which means that your attention is established to be free of trying to defend yourself, and you have refused to convince or persuade others of your point of view. If you watch people around you will notice that they spend 99% of their time trying to defend their points of view.

When you are on the defensive, blaming others and not accepting the moment, you will also face defenses against you. Every time you face a defensive action you must recognize that if you force the situation, this defense against you will continue to increase.

David, the "killer of giants", was a great winner because he understood this concept. The Holy Scriptures say that while King David was entering the gate of Bahurim, one of his cities, a man named Shimei cursed him and threw stones at him. Then Abishai, one of his soldiers, said to him:

— Why should this dead dog curse my lord the king? Please, let me go over and take off his head!

But David responded:
— Leave him alone, and let him curse…. It may be that the Lord will look on my affliction, and that the Lord will repay me with good for his cursing this day.

David understood that for a winner, through the principle of resistance, the curses of the enemies become the blessings of the master.

So, does it mean winners do not fight evil? Of course they do, but they have no personal interests in the battle. Having denied selfish conveniences, winners align themselves with the forces of truth, goodness, beauty, compassion, equanimity, and harmony, and surpass the darkness by bringing the light. Even if they face enormous impossibilities, they understand that it is their implicit responsibility to face and accept the challenges that this world presents to them.

As a winner, you must give up completely your wish to defend your point of view. When you have no point to defend, you will not allow the birth of an argument. In my case, that day I did the opposite.

—*I know what to do so this individual will not bother us any more* —I replied to Yarissette, slamming the table and continuing one of the most absurd phrases I had been taught—. *He will know that no one messes with God's children.*

— *What will we do?* — she asked, startled.

—*I will sue him for defamation and damages.*

— *Great!* — Yari answered with a smile.

I immediately called a pastor friend in Baltimore, I knew that his church was attended by influential lawyers from Washington DC.

—*I need your best lawyer* — was the phrase with which I opened the phone conversation. Following this I explained what the problem was about.

— *Two years ago, something similar happened to me. I have the ideal person* — he said as he searched the information in his database—. *Here it is. Michael Brown, the best lawsuit lawyer in the city of Washington.*

I felt the blood rush through my veins. I was eager to give this guy a lesson.

At the end of the conversation, I immediately called the lawyer's cell phone, told him about the recommendation, and explained the problem to him. The next day I was in Washington sitting in his office with Yarissette.

—*'I have to be honest, it will not be an easy task. The first thing to do is to know who this individual is, what his last name is, in what city he lives. I tried to investigate yesterday but his blog does not have any information,* —said the lawyer, explaining that a blog is not a formal website, therefore anyone can create it, even with false information—. *All you need is an email which you can also acquire under any name.* —he continued— *When we find him, we will submit a lawsuit for damages worth one million dollars.*

— *What is the first step?* —I asked.
— *Hire a private investigator and do all our inquiries. For this I need a legal retainer of ten thousand dollars.*

—*Done* —I replied with a certain sense of satisfaction, and he gave me the contract he had already prepared.

The first task was to find out what his last name was.

—*We will answer every call this time*— I suggested to Yarissette, and he agreed that in a subtle way we would find out his last name. In fact, days later he called again.

—*What agreement do you want to make, how would I pay you?" What's more, how can I make arrangements with you if I do not even know your last name?* —I asked him during one of the conversations.

—*Rodriguez. William Rodriguez* —he answered and gave me a number where I could call him.

The private investigator began to work with this information. It turned out to be a South Carolina number in his wife's name. He found out his address through the telephone company and this was all we needed. Days later he had been notified of the one-million-dollar lawsuit for defamation and damages.

I would never have imagined the damage I was causing myself.

Defense fuels the fire of a battle. Resistance demonstrates your ability to endure. Defense is based on protecting who we are. Resistance is the indefectible death of the ego. The one who dies to the illusory idea of the image being reborn into freedom.

Today I understand more than ever Jesus' proposal: *"You have heard that it was said, 'Eye for eye, and tooth for tooth.' But I tell you... If anyone slaps you on the right cheek, turn to them the other cheek as well"*.

Years later I would realize that defending myself generates more violence and only peace exterminates war. Victorious individuals understand that violent behavior is nothing more than the result of a deep need for attention and love. Recognizing this, I now understand that I should not have allowed myself retribution or feel the need to pass judgment, knowing that people are doing the best they can from their level of consciousness.

Victorious individuals do not fight or push others towards their ideals. Rather, they strive to have the ability to understand the behavior pattern of the opponent, evaluate the condition that leads them to do what they do, and look for a creative way to solve the problem.

Winners know that a high ego means lack of love; it is a limited sense of being, it does not allow real love to exist and it diminishes life. Violence and evil are literally the perversion of love, lost love, and a desperate need to recover it.

Compassion is a living emotion that vibrates within victorious individuals and connects with those around them.

To see the world from others' perspective means to undertake the plane of their emotions, to understand the world through their eyes. This is the true power of resistance. Compassion, courage, and creativity empower a victorious individual and motivate all his or her intentions and actions. Like the great prophets of history, they commit themselves to the highest ideals we value as civilization.

From a practical perspective, these great characters are a representation of ourselves. Their ability to feel compassion and emanate love is also part of our collective belief system. But more than that, these skills are an intrinsic aspect of our potential as human beings. We all have the ability to cultivate the principle of resistance and see how compassion can change our lives.

Resistance is creativity

"Our thoughts, acts, and needs are the thread with which we sew our own net".

The paradox of our existence is that we are also the only species in which members go to war with each other, perpetuate horrible crimes against each other, institutionalize tribal alliances (in the Name of God) and carry out technological advances and scientific innovations for the most diabolical purposes. Historical winners have seen this as the result of the need for understanding and love, which is expressed in many ways. Yet, their response to friction never fails; they face conflict by fulfilling their needs with creativity.

Over the years I came to realize that problems are not solved with confrontation but rather with creativity. Creativity is an integral part of the principle of resistance, therefore, winners recognize that their essence is pure creativity.

Before we go any further, let us begin by understanding exactly what creativity is. Creativity is a dimension in which our spirit brings new meanings and contexts to any situation or problem that occurs.

New meanings are manifested when there is a change in our perspective. When you interpret a problem as an opportunity, there is a change of meaning. A new context appears when there is a change in the understanding of the relationships that operate in the situation.

If I had perceived William's action at that moment not as an attack, but as an opportunity for my maturity to grow, my reaction would have been very different, surely saving myself years of headaches. Therefore, our reactions depend entirely on the way in which we perceive and understand an issue.

The story of Joseph in the Bible has been one of the most fascinating to me since I was a child. This young man, who I would also call a winner, faced great challenges in his life, including the betrayal of his own brothers. He decided not to look at these overwhelming challenges as problems, but as opportunities. In fact, years after the terrible betrayal of his brothers, he finds them again. When they realized it was Joseph, they feared for their lives, since Joseph had become one of the most powerful men of his time, but on the contrary, these were the words of Joseph: *"I am your brother Joseph, the one you sold into Egypt! And now, do not be distressed and do not be angry with yourselves for selling me here, because it was to save lives that God sent me ahead of you."*

Winners do not lose control over a difficult situation. Since the word "problem" is not part of their vocabulary, they only see challenges as opportunities.

Every action has a reaction. The battle you are facing right now can make a big turn in your favor or against you. It all depends on the action you take today. I hope your action is one of resistance and not of defense.

Defense creates in itself an opposite atmosphere that feeds on a protest.

—*You think you are smart, but I am smarter than you. You are going to hear from me very soon* —William said, after a heated conversation about the lawsuit.

—*I hope so* — I answered ironically, hanging up the phone.

A few weeks later, a policeman was knocking on my door. Surprised, I asked: — *How can I help you?*

— *I'm Detective Owens, I'd like to ask Mr. Dionny Baez a few questions.*

Astutely, William had prepared a counter-lawsuit. The same one that would ignite all the chaos that unfolded in the next few years. The same one that I would have saved myself from if I had waited without counterattacking.
Today I can say I have learned that it is better to die to your ego, because: Who can fight against a dead person? He who dies to himself finds no opposition. He who dies to himself can enjoy his present.

If you do this consistently, if you stop fighting and defending yourself, you will fully experience the present, which is a gift. Someone once told me: "the past is history, the future is a mystery, and this moment is a gift. This is why we call this-moment 'present'. If I had truly understood that concept, I would not have to have lived the battle that would ensue afterwards.

Applying the principle of Resistance

I will activate the principle of resistance in my life by committing myself to taking the following steps:

1. Today I will take a few minutes to pray. I will accept things as they are right now, not as I wish they were.

2. By accepting things as they are, I will take responsibility of all the events I perceive as problems, not blaming myself or blaming people or issues. Rather, I will make myself responsible of transforming my problems into opportunities.

3. Today I am prepared to not defend myself, and I will surrender the need to convince others of my point of view. I am free from retaliation.

3

The Principle
of
RECONDITIONING

T errified by Detective Owens' questions and after making some inquiries, I called Michael immediately, my lawsuit's solicitor.

—*Apparently William has invented something new. The worst of it all is that he got the law involved and is not alone* —I said. Surprised by the news Michael explained that it would be wise to hire a lawyer in Philadelphia to take care of the problem. When it was resolved, Michael would continue with what we had initiated.

—*I have to fly to Puerto Rico tomorrow and then to Guatemala, but when I return I will do that* —I answered.

The next day I was on a plane. An influential Puerto Rican female pastor, whom I had met recently, had invited me to participate in the "Young Torch" congress to share a few lectures. Even at that moment I had no idea of the aggressiveness that would characterize the battle. William had already contacted the offices in Puerto Rico.

—*There is a man who has not stopped calling and is asking us to cancel your participation, he says he will create a scandal otherwise* —the pastor said, as she laughed. Of course, she would not grant his request. She could not imagine what was about to happen.

Five days later, one thousand five hundred and sixty-eight miles south-west of Puerto Rico, in Zacapa, a hot Guatemala town, the cell phone kept ringing.

— *Dionny, this is David Velasquez, are you okay?*
— *Yes of course. What happened?* — I answered, while other calls were coming in.
— *You were on TV just now.*

William had managed to strike once more. This time he contacted a famous TV show in Puerto Rico. He said he knew that a certain influential pastor had recent had friction with the program and negative news would be appealing to them.

— *They say you're in prison* — David continued—, *that you live in Puerto Rico and that you work with the pastor you were with last week.*

It was the ideal gossip! The news ran like fire. I got calls from all over. Now I faced three dilemmas: the legal action he had brought on, the police complaint and a piece of gossip that gradually worsened through the media and included a second person who had nothing to do with the issue.

Who was to blame? Superficially we could say that William was. But the truth is, the culprit was myself.

In my eagerness to demonstrate that I was right, I created a legal situation that would never have existed if I had not first filed the lawsuit. However, without realizing my great mistake, I did it again on a larger scale. I tried to sue the TV show as well. An international program with a lot of power. This attempt to sue the TV program created greater confrontation. Now I would become the target of a second enemy unnecessarily, since the demand against the program would never proceed. "Apparently and allegedly" was the phrase with which the producer opened the program, this means that after this sentence he could say anything about anyone without fear of being sued for defamation. Again, through my counterattack, I had won a new an even worse enemy.

The roots of war are usually invisible. These roots feed on the mental conditioning that creates the highest levels of toxicity in a person's life. The most powerful conditioning exists in the more subtler levels of the mind. These begin in the early years of a child's life, while an infant's brain learns how to think, feel, and behave according to the influences he or she receives at home. Conditioning has become a dominant feature in us since we were still infants.

It is in those moments that we establish patterns in our brains for life. Even today you are reviving scenarios that you learned when you were two or three years old. Consider a child who has gone out with her mother. She sees a giant lollypop and wants it. What does she do? The most common pattern is the following: First, she asks her mother in a very tender way, she asks her in a sweet voice if mom wants to buy her a lollypop. If this tactic does not work, she tries the opposite, acting unpleasantly. She complains, cries and creates a whole drama. If this does not work, the next step is to act rebelliously and indifferently. She refuses to obey her mother, who wants her to calm down and stop being difficult. If rebellion does not work, the last scenario is to act as a victim: poor me, nobody loves me enough to buy me a lollypop. When the mother finally gives up, the child is conditioned, thinking that she has discovered something that "works".

Millions of adults around the world continue to act within this emotional cycle, using the same tactic to achieve what they want, as they believe it "works". The problem with this conditioning is that by manipulating others, you will never receive what you want, which is greater love, peace, and joy. Because this type of conditioning trains the brain to a false sense of happiness, you are really manipulating yourself. You become the kind of person who always wants to get away with it and be right, even if it costs you peace in the process.

Winners have realized that true peace is the product of mental re-conditioning that leads them to surrender the need to get away with something and to get everyone to see that they were right.

Being right implies that someone else must be wrong. Every relationship is damaged by the confrontation of who is right and who is not.

The result is great suffering and conflict in the world. Surrendering the need to prove that you are right does not mean that you do not have a point of view, but that your happiness is not bound to others accepting it or not. To achieve this, a re-conditioning is necessary. Thus, clearing the toxic behaviors we learned as children, to enter a no-defense state where you will become invincible, because there is nothing to attack.

Being a victim depends on your perception

"If you never assume importance, you will never lose it".

Most people live trying to impose their views on the world. The statement: "I am right" brings comfort, but not true happiness. From that mentality, those who you feel have offended you will never apologize or make your wounds disappear. The people you judge will always stay away from you. No one has been happy just by proving that he or she was right. The only result is conflict and confrontation. And this was exactly what I was going through.

The coming months were devastating. Yarissette and I did not want to answer the phone for fear that a new story would come out on the television, while we fought against them with any other means we could wherein they were wrong. The never-ending battle of seeing who could get away with it. I still did not realize that my attitude only made the battle more critical.

When our need to show that we are right disappears, we will not have more grievances and resentment, which are the result of showing that someone else is wrong. The only thing that creates victims is the personal perception of what is wrong. But there are no real victims in the world, only people who have received terrible injustices and who have been devastated. Injustice is very real and undeniable. But the title "victim", is something totally different. It is a psychological wound. A person who has been scarred and has not been healed can only build a story reinforced by each new experience: "I have been hurt by life, my situation is painful. I am resentful of those who hurt me. My pain has become who I am". In the end, being a victim is really a form of prejudice against yourself. In the name of being hurt, you hurt yourself every day by taking on the role of victim.

Among the winners in these fascinating biblical stories there are two that to this day constantly resonate with me. The story of Jesus and of course, how could I forget Paul; the "more than conqueror". Paul superficially possessed all the experience necessary to consider himself a victim of fate and tyrants. In fact, in one of his letters he writes the following:

"From the Jews five times I received forty stripes minus one. Three times I was beaten with rods; once I was stoned; three times I was shipwrecked; a night and a day I have been in the deep; in journeys often, in perils of waters, in perils of robbers, in perils of my own countrymen, in perils of the Gentiles, in perils in the city, in perils in the wilderness, in perils in the sea, in perils among false brethren; in weariness and toil, in sleeplessness often, in hunger and thirst, in fastings often, in cold and nakedness— In Damascus the governor, under Aretas the king, was guarding the city of the Damascenes with a garrison, desiring to arrest me; but I was let down in a basket through a window in the wall, and escaped from his hands."

(2 Corinthians 11:24-27, 32, 33)

He was affected by great injustices and exuberant rejections his entire life. His very death could be considered synonymous with total failure.

The story tells that when Paul was to be beheaded, he turned to the east, raised

70

his hands to heaven and wept with emotion as he prayed in his own language and gave thanks to God for a long time; then said goodbye to the Christians who were present, knelt with both knees on the ground, and blindfolded his eyes with a veil which he had borrowed from a woman named Plautila while walking to the place of the torture so the executioner would cover his eyes. He put his neck on the gash and from this position he was beheaded immediately. Even in his very death, in that manner, Paul teaches us, among many other things, that we are but simple bricks of a building; or branches from a tree; or members of a body: all figures used by him to show us that personal goals, with the achievements and goals that we consider normal, are not precisely the climax of our existence.

That is why, while through our human eyes we see him as a humiliated prisoner, dragging chains with his sore feet, subject to the will of rude and cruel soldiers, and anything that might characterize defeat and weakness, he saw something far beyond that. He saw himself as victorious, someone for whom none of these circumstances could rob him of the inner peace and the assurance that he was on the right path. It was from this state of being and assurance that he wrote the following, from one of his prisons:

"Who shall separate us from the love of Christ? Shall tribulation, or distress, or persecution, or famine, or nakedness, or peril, or sword? Yet in all these things we are more than conquerors through Him who loved us".

(Romans 8:35, 37)

Indeed, he was not a victim. His conviction and example of life affirmed to millions of believers that would come in future generations, which is to be more than a conqueror.

Giving up resentment disconnects you from anger and hostility. Anger closes the door to the dimension of the spirit. Even if you feel that it is very justifiable to circle your wounds, on a deeper level you have tied yourself to the one who hurt you. That connection becomes so important that it obscures the connection with the spirit.

So many times, have we used spirituality to justify our moral strife against the injustice of the world. However, this is still aggressiveness, and the result is that more anger, resentment, and hostility are added to the battle.

Winners who really fight the injustice in the world are not consumed by quarreling. They have a clear mind, self-control, and self-assurance in their values of life. They can distinguish between the past, where which nothing can be done, and the present, which is therefore, amendable.

Re-condition your level of consciousness

"No problem can be solved from the same level of consciousness that created it".

Einstein

To be victorious it is necessary to recondition our mind to higher levels. Whenever you try to rationalize your anger as justifiable, remember that self-justification causes a deeper antagonism.

The level of the solution will always be different to the level of the problem.

To go beyond the level of a problem, you must clearly see yourself. At that moment, I could not see that what I was defending was my need to be right. This attitude is very subtle, because the signs are not always anger and resentment. But self-justification always has a common denominator: refusing to surrender. Only by surrendering we are free from prejudice. When you are dominated by your ego, surrender feels like total defeat. Your ego is strengthened under these conditions:

- *You always achieve what you want*
- *Others must agree to follow your schedule*
- *There is a sense of control*
- *Everyone must acknowledge your truth*

The higher levels of the spirit are only accessed when the winner surrenders. The secret is not in surrendering to another person or to each other. The winner surrenders to purpose. The shared purpose. Your commitment is not to what you want. Individual desires are secondary. Your commitment is to the purpose, and to wherever it is taking you. In this way, you surrender your egocentric perspective. Your approach is re-conditioned to the place between you and what you perceive as an opponent. This is the space between the ego and the spirit. Every time you are tempted to obey your ego,

go to this space and ask yourself the following:
In which of my decisions will I show more love?
What will bring the most peace?
What does God want to show me through this?
Could I give without expecting anything in return?

These questions have no automatic answers. They serve rather to awaken you spiritually. They synchronize you with a process that is larger than "you" and "me". The advantages of doing this are not obvious at first. Your past conditioning will say, "What's wrong with achieving what I want? Why should I consider another person even when he or she acts unfairly? I have the right to have people see the truth".

What your ego cannot see is something more precious, hidden in this spiritual principle: mystery. The mystery that is born out of love and takes you to a place of peace and joy that is not tied to present situations, because you know that there is a greater purpose that must be manifested. In my case, I had to experience a lot before I conceived this concept.

Days passed and the battle became more acute, all sorts of stories and conclusions surfaced on the internet, while my ego struggled. On the other hand, the legal complaint that William had formulated to counter the lawsuit took a more serious, unexpected turn every day, of which I did not realize. Today I understand that before arriving at a total re-conditioning, the pressure of life must take us to a point where returning becomes almost impossible.

Hooke's law is a technical term that describes the tendency of materials to return to their original state after the pressure has been removed. For example, when a piece of metal has been heated, it expands. After the heat has been removed, the metal returns to its original condition. This law has taken place.

Something similar happens with humans. Most often individuals return to their original state when a new force is no longer applied. You remember where you were before that force came and you return to that familiar place.

To create a permanent change within a material (or a human being), a force must be applied that exceeds the "elastic limit" of the object, or the old conditioning of the individual. How can you transcend and introduce yourself to new levels in your life? The purpose must be so strong that it dominates your thoughts, your decisions, your activities, and even your immediate dreams. The pressure's forcefulness will determine the size of your purpose and your ability to evolve will determine how long you will live under pressure.

Destruction is creation

"If people knew how hard I worked to achieve my mastery, it wouldn't seem so wonderful after all".

Michelangelo

Deep in my soul I hoped that something good would result from such evil.

That day would be one of the most shocking to me. Once again, I had to travel to Puerto Rico, this time, for a press conference. The afternoon had taken us by surprise as we tried to fight the humid heat of the island. After a busy day, we arrived at Rafi's house, who was my coordinator at that time.

— *How about a lemonade to freshen up?*

—*Great* — I answered, while we sat in a small patio at the back of his house. It would have been around six in the afternoon. Through the glass doors leading to the inner room we could watch the TV.

— Shall we watch your favorite program?

I knew that Rafi, in joking terms, alluded to the program with which I had the confrontation. They had not mentioned me for a few days, and I really hoped it would not continue. But to my surprise, that was not the case.

The coolness of the night began to seep through the slow breeze. Everything seemed to be going well. Hector Febres and Luis Calderon, two friends who helped with our promotional tour, accompanied us. Rafi had served the lemonade, and between jokes and laughter I pretended to listen attentively to the conversation. The truth was, I was paying more attention to the program that had already started minutes before. In the distance, behind the glass doors you could see the program, although I did not hear what they were saying. And suddenly there it was. An unpleasant shiver invaded my inside as I once again saw my photo on television. It was as if time had stopped. My expression of displeasure was surely what alerted the others, who stopped talking and turned to the television.

—*Oh man* — were Rafi's words as he opened the doors to hear clearly what they were saying. The dialogue was between the producer and the program's presenter.

—*Shall I say it?*
—*Bring it out* —the presenter said.
After repeating the same dynamic for a few seconds, the producer finally broke the news.
—*Ladies and gentlemen, now. Show the paper.*
Something similar to a legal order appeared on the screen.
—*Dionny Baez will have to appear before a court in the next few days...* —while the producer continued, my cell phone began to vibrate.
—*You should be watching the television...* —as if it were not enough, it was William, who not only managed to officially start a trial against me, but also publish it on international television.

After a heated and unpleasant conversation, I hung up the phone to immediately call Yarissette, who had stayed in Philadelphia this time. In a choppy, nervous voice, she wondered what we were going to do, because we had never been serious about William's complaint, we did not have a lawyer in Philadelphia to represent us, and some detectives had already been asking about me. Jumping from his seat and with the cell phone in his hand Rafi was sure he knew the right person.

Richie Miranda was his name. A lawyer friend who supposedly knew many people of influence. After calling him, in less than forty minutes he was there.

—This is Dionny Baez, the person I have been telling you about, —Rafi said. Richie was already familiar with my name, in fact, a lot of people in Puerto Rico were, after the great scandal unfolded.

After a detailed explanation of the situation, Richie held out his hand to me and said:
—I think I can help you. Tomorrow I'm going to Philadelphia, I have some friends there. You should wait here in Puerto Rico for a few days until I have resolved everything.
We spent the rest of the night looking for strategies to counteract the attack. Indeed, Richie was in Philadelphia the next day.

Until now, I do not know for sure how Richie found Jamie, the young Jew who would later become my lawyer. All I know is that Jamie was supposed to belong to a prestigious law firm specializing in defamation, which represented high-ranking city officials, what he needed was $ 13,000 to begin with, ensuring that everything would be all right. Given the emergence of the situation, Yarissette did not hesitate to find the money and give it to Richie. I decided to wait two more days and travel from Puerto Rico to Boston, where I had my next conference. When it was over, I was on my way to my home town.

It was springtime in Philadelphia. The drastic change in temperature was a surprise to me along with the realization that Jamie was not the lawyer Richie said he was, worse, the thirteen thousand dollars never reached his hands. When we looked for Richie ... he had vanished.

Applying the principle of Re-conditioning:

I will activate the principle of re-conditioning in my life by committing myself to take the next steps:

1. Today I will take a few minutes to pray, and will meditate on the way I persuade others to get what I want.
2. I agree not to manipulate people or situations.
3. As for my battle, I will answer the following questions:
In which of my decisions will I show more love?
What will bring peace?
What does God want to show me through this?
Could I give without expecting anything in return?

Book Two

Yarissette

The power of defamation overwhelms you, clouds your senses, makes you feel helpless before the shadows of lies, and tends to easily distort your reality.

For some years I have been asked: "As a wife and as a woman, how could you face such a battle?"

I think there will never be a simple answer. However, in the next chapters I will try as honestly as possible to answer the question and therefore, add to the principles that my husband has exposed in the previous three chapters. From my experience, I would like to begin with the principle of clarity.

The Principle of
CLARITY

C armen Lidia was the name her parents chose. The girl was born in a remote field of a very small town in Puerto Rico. They were extremely poor, had a very little budget and half a dozen children.

Soon though, the pressure of necessity would bring her parents into an interminable confrontation that would form part of her childhood. The latent memories of constant verbal and physical abuse between her parents were revived again and again until her adolescence. Without finding an apparent solution, her mother chose to channel this anger towards her children, thus, worsening the situation.

At the age of eighteen, Carmen met Reinaldo Gonzalez, a handsome young man who seemed to have a deep spirituality and a bright future, the same young man with whom she would flee later with the hope of running away from the hell she lived in, just to fall into a worse one.

Apparently, her life was about to take a turn for the worse.

As if someone had written the script of the most horrifying film to later be reproduced, each of the patterns was repeated, with the only difference in this reproduction is that the chaos would be greater.

Influenced by evil associates, Reinaldo decided to indulge in drugs and alcohol, so his days were tarnished by the darkness of not knowing what the young Carmen Lidia would have to expect when Reinaldo returned home. She knew she had to flee once more, as if with closed eyes she jumped into the unknown once again, embarking on a journey with no return, but with the hope of finding peace. But again, and again, she was motionless, with the terror of tomorrow's uncertainty.

Under the hostile atmosphere of innumerable mistreatment and unexplained abuse, her first child was born, probably destined to repeat the dark cycles that had disturbed her family.

Her firstborn would be the only one of the three children to remember her father living at home. The event that would distress her life had its outcome under the gray sky of the raw winter of nineteen eighty-nine. The five-year-old girl with her three little siblings: Amanda, two years old, Emelisa, one-year old, and little baby Emmanuel who was barely alive in Carmen's womb, were finally thrown out of the house.

— *Where are we going, mommy?* —the girl repeated with a mix of tears and fear as she clung to Carmen Lidia's dress. Although the other two girls could not speak, the desperation of their cries did not need words, the trauma of what had just happened was been very strong.

An hour before, Carmen Lidia had come home after a church service. This time, Reinaldo had arrived a little earlier than usual, and as expected he was drunk and stoned. She slowly opened the door, praying to the Lord that Reinaldo had not arrived first; this time for some strange reason God did not answer her prayer. Like a wild cat Reinaldo jumped out of the darkness.

— *Who are you fooling around with?* —Reinaldo yelled, gritting his teeth as if he were forgetting that Carmen Lidia was about to give birth, and that she was still carrying little Emelisa in her arms. She knew he would not hit the baby, so hiding behind her again and again she tried to explain that she was coming back from church.

The screams of the girls seemed to enrage the man even more, who was insistently screaming more frantically.

—I know someone else got you pregnant. That baby is not mine. You leave this house today, grab your things and get out.

Seeking to survive the attack, Carmen Lidia took advantage of the space and ran with her three girls to the room. She quickly closed the door, but she knew the door would not stand the blows of a drugged and enraged man.

—Give me wisdom, Lord, what shall I do? — Immediately, the image of her sister Eva came to mind.

— If I stay here, he is going to kill me.
Without thinking twice and without time to take any of their belongings, Carmen Lidia shouted:
— Okay, I am going to leave the room. I am leaving, but do not hurt me.

When she did not hear an answer, she took her three little ones and quickly left the house thinking of staying at her sister's house. A difficult trip, not only because it was late and it had snowed, but because the trek was long, she had no car and the girls were too small to walk.

The five-year-old got her shoes wet in the cold since she was the oldest and walked; and, between cries of desperation, they faced a daunting task.

Amanda and Emelisa were too small to remember what happened, too small to miss the presence of their father during childhood, too small to relive those raw memories. Memories that would impact the firstborn for life.

It was not easy for the five-year-old girl, or for the small family, who would have to go through the rest of their lives without a father's presence. Carmen Lidia would have to accept the two roles, roles that she really executed very well.

What would become of that first-born?

Anyone would say that the five-year-old would be destined to repeat the same cycles of past generations and I agree. But today the little girl lives happily because at an early age she learned to forgive.

Today I can write about that little girl and teach about forgiveness because that little one... was me.

My life experience taught me at first instance that the worst losers are those who fight their battles from the land of wounds.

The biggest winners have reached their victories because their battles are strategic.

Correct strategies naturally flow into a mind that enjoys clarity, and clarity is impossible if it is influenced by the toxic flows produced by unforgiveness.

This same clarity led me to be strategic at the end of the battle that my husband and I had to face later. Although I must admit that at first, I was very tempted to act with resentment.

Forgiveness is clarity

"Not forgiving is like drinking a poison and waiting for the other person to die".

Biblical winners have refused to dwell on the emotions that could cloud their clarity; their sound mind provided as a result the fundamental strategies with which they have won their worst battles.

Among these victorious individuals, one of my favorite stories has always been Queen Esther's.

Esther lived during the period when the Persians dominated all of western Asia and Egypt. They imposed a high degree of conquest through violence in their vast empire.

Her story happened almost 600 years before the birth of Christ. After the destruction of Jerusalem, the Jews were taken captive to Babylon and Esther's parents were among them. The Jewish girl grew up orphaned and homeless, but ended up raised by an older relative, her uncle and adoptive father, Mordecai. No doubt, she was a perfect candidate for resentment and unforgiveness. However, this story shows a brave spirit willing to forgive her parents' aggressors in order to fulfill a greater purpose.

Esther was very beautiful, and she had to be, for King Ahasuerus had labored to make his Persian empire known and sought after because it had the most beautiful women. Among such beauties, Esther was considered to compete against other maidens for the King's favor. But who would want the favor of someone who represented past aggressions? This would otherwise have been rejected unless there had been a deep conviction that the worst battles were won through forgiveness and that resentment only produces turbulence and a lack of clarity. When all the ceremonies were finished, her beauty proved to be superior and to the surprise of everyone, she took the throne becoming the wife of the King. As she was intelligent and sensitive, and thanks to her uncle Mordecai, she discovered a plan that was being worked out by Haman to kill the Jews. As I looked more closely at Haman's past, I realized that he acted out of resentment. Like Esther, his ancestors were also killed, but this time the perpetrators were the same Jews. He was an Amalekite and centuries before a Jewish king named Saul had tried to exterminate them by killing men, women, and children.

Haman was the second authority in the kingdom under the command of King Ahasuerus and had ordered that, after his highness, he had to be heard and respected. The king did not have enough interest to investigate the details, so he appointed Haman to act on his behalf, and gave him his ring declaring Haman to be the executive authority and do as he pleased. Haman promptly prepared the edict, copied it, translated it, sealed it with the king's ring, and sent it to the whole empire by means of a postal system inaugurated by Cyrus.

Esther understood that it was no coincidence that she had been named queen, but that she had to do something to save her people.

On the third day Esther put into action her purpose. Calm and majestic in her royal dress, standing in the inner courtyard at some distance from the throne, she approached the king. The king extended his golden scepter to his consort as she approached him. He asked her what the problem was, which had brought her to the king's presence.

The king invited her to ask for half of the kingdom, a non-literal expression. Esther was content to invite him to a private party prepared for the king and Haman, in which he would present her with an opportunity to make her true request.

The promptness with which the king sent for Haman shows that Esther's invitation had pleased him. Esther, had to prepare in advance for the banquet, anticipating the acceptance of the king. The king was in a good mood, ready to give her whatever she asked for.

Esther presented her petition to the king: May my life be granted ... and that of my people. These petitions were surprising in their implications and guaranteed the king's full attention.

Using the passive to avoid naming Amman at that time, Esther referred to the immense amount by which the Jews had essentially been sold. Having been sold into slavery could have been tolerated, but the same verbs used in the decree were exchanged for those to be destroyed, killed and exterminated. No amount of money could compensate for the loss the king would suffer if the Jewish people were exterminated. Esther appealed to the king's best interests and suggested that people are far more important than possessions.

The king discovers that Haman was responsible for the plot to kill his queen and her people; in his anger, he took a moment to reflect while deciding how to handle this situation. Haman in his haste only thought of begging the queen to have mercy on him. Forgetting the customary protocol, he got too close to the queen, further enraging the king. The eunuchs at the service of the king apprehended and covered Haman's face, which practically meant they were arresting him. Haman, without knowing it, had made the preparations for his own execution, which was carried out immediately. The anger of the king was appeased because justice had been done. While Haman's decree had caused dismay, he completely changed their destinies, ending up dead in the gallows that he himself had prepared for the Jews. Esther could have chosen not to forgive the Persians and hate them for her entire life, but of course, she would never have been queen and, without a doubt, would have lost her life along with her people. The story of Haman shows us that we usually end up hung up with the resentment we prepare for our enemies.

Although many of us do not find ourselves in this kind of circumstance, there are certainly endless things we could live resentful with ... a neighbor's dog, government taxes, not receiving our salary on time, traffic, a husband who leaves the lid of the toilet open and his underwear on the bathroom floor. Also, children who do not show appreciation for everything you do for them. Then, there are people who will say bad things and never apologize, parents who never show affection, favoritism among siblings, false accusations, and the list goes on into an endless cascade of opportunities to continue being angry or to forgive and move on. In a way, I empathize with Esther, because someone who attacks your marriage is also fighting against the life of your future generations. But, how can you effectively protect your destiny? This question can only be answered from a state of clarity that has not been overshadowed by hurt and resentment.

I realized on that day at the beach in Atlantic City when we got the call that would start it all that this was very important for our emotional stability and unity in this battle. The marked extortion to which we were exposed and how defamation evolved, undoubtedly taught me that the enemy was not in our house but outside, developing a full conviction within our marriage and a sense of belonging that prompted us not to give up. At the same time, that same sense of belonging is what tends to tempt you to act with resentment, which we honestly did at the beginning of our battle.

Because we had acted resentfully now we had a legal problem that would escalate to unimaginable dimensions, while at the same time we had to deal with the shame of being defamed by an international program, attacked viciously on the internet, be rejected by those who claimed to be our friends, suffer prejudice from people, receive doubts from family members and the people we loved, our trips and events canceled, our finances in chaos, and as if that were not enough, the theft of thirteen thousand dollars by Richie Miranda. In fact, these were very difficult things to forgive.

Our natural reaction was hate, hurt, anger, resentment and unforgiveness.

But who are we really hurting with these negative emotions? The person who committed the offense? Sometimes it hurts people when we take them out of our lives through spite, but usually they do not even know we are angry! And we walk around worried about our anger, remembering the offense again and again. How much time have you spent imagining what you are going to say to the person who offended you, while you enrage yourself even more? When we allow ourselves to do this, we hurt ourselves. In the end, we feel mistreated much more than the one who offended us. When Jamie -the young lawyer- learned that Richie had used the situation to steal from us, he burst out in frustration.

— *I never got the money!* — Jamie said, surprised. *But I understand that I was as guilty as you were, we should have made the deal personally and not have used a third party. You have two options, you can find another lawyer and start from scratch, or hire me.*

My husband knew that Jamie had already made the relevant inquiries and looking for another lawyer would involve taking more time in the process, time which we did not have. On the other hand, I had also realized that Jamie had no experience in this type of case, but we decided to take the risk.

—*OK. Let's do it. Let's start the process* — Dionny said.

That night, the tension increased with every second. Two months had passed and in only hours we would have our first trial. The month of October of two thousand seven. We spent the entire night hanging around. An army of questions continually attacked me: Will we meet William today? What perception will the Judge have? Who else will be involved in this? Deep inside I felt that an endless number of surprises awaited us.

The light rays of the sun crept through the curtains of our bedroom, announcing that it was morning. There was no time to lose.

Peace gives us clarity, anger weakens us

"Anger and intolerance are the enemies of correct understanding".

Mahatma Gandhi

We both got up before the alarm sounded, a sign that we had not slept all night. The truth is, we did not say much that morning, maybe because we were too nervous to talk. Two hours later, in the building of the Court of Philadelphia, we opened for the first time the doors of that depressing room. It was completely plated with reddish wood, four long benches of the same material spread from door to door, and at the end, it was marked with the Pennsylvania shield, the stand where the judge would sit stood majestically. After a few minutes, we heard for the first time that voice in English:

—*Honorable Judge Harold Kane, all stand.* A gray-haired, white man in his sixties, dressed in a black robe and entered the room. After some procedures, I heard a statement that made my body shiver.

— *Dionny Baez vs. the Commonwealth of Pennsylvania.* A woman with an aggressive spirit, who showed she knew the system well, started the discussion. It was the prosecutor hired to argue the case against us. Taking out a long list and after reading my husband's name once more, she began to mention the charges she considered should be applicable according to the plot they had prepared. To our surprise, William was not there.

Holding on to my husband's hand, I assured him that none of the charges would proceed. They seemed ridiculous to me, and apparently to the judge too. Immediately the judge overruled most of them, allowing us to fight only two. Even though we had somehow won in that first encounter, I was livid because I knew that everything had not ended there. The entire following year we would be presenting ourselves again and again without any progress, the judge would not arrive or the trial would be postponed for some absurd reason while we continued to face the multifaceted confrontation of defamation and finger pointing every day from those who, without any idea of what was happening, accused us without mercy. How difficult it is to forgive. In these situations, it is very common to fall into the anger trap, which, when repressed, becomes the hatred that subtly consumes us.

Medical studies have shown that hatred causes everything from ulcers to bad temper. At the very least, it is a waste of precious time. Every hour that we are angry is an hour that we have used and that we will never have back.

The people we need to forgive usually do not deserve it and sometimes they do not care. Maybe they do not even know they hurt us.

Repressed anger turns into hatred, and hatred can quickly turn into anger. Anger is dangerous. In this state, people can do all sorts of things that could alter the rest of their lives.

Because of the frustration in which we lived, I noticed that my character was changing. Over the next few months I abruptly began to disconnect from our friends, even those who sincerely loved us. I just wanted to make our aggressor paid for what we were going through. I learned that living angry at something or someone only distorts our vision in battle, leads us to make the worst decisions and limits us to judge people or situations under the same frustration of what we are going through.

When we experience the hatred or anger of someone against us, it often involves much more than the situation that occurred. We can be driving and see someone angry at us because we did not use the appropriate signal. Their anger was disproportionate to the offense: we made a small mistake and they are so angry they want to hurt us, but even if their anger is directed at us, it is not really about us. It is a tally of perhaps years of unresolved problems in their lives.

Today we heard of a gunman who entered a building shooting a lot of people, killing some and injuring others. Under rage, this person began shooting at people he did not even know. Why? His anger increased to uncontrollable and violent rage.

How many people are in prison today because they killed someone while in anger? How many ruined or seriously damaged relationships because they said damaging, hurtful things, while angry? We then conclude that while forgiveness produces clarity to make better decisions in your battle, anger blinds your understanding.

My mother used to always say one Biblical verse to me: *"The wise woman builds her house, but the foolish pulls it down with her hands."* I knew that if I wanted to see victory in this battle I would have to think clearly; but in particular, I needed to help my husband do the same. I understood that it was time to return to that place of tranquility and apply those concepts that once led me to forgive my father, during the most critical moments of my adolescence.

Forgiveness is a process

"To forgive, you must deny yourself".

Publio Nasón.

It is easy to tell a person "you have to forgive those who have hurt you". But what if they don't know how to do it?

Through my experience, I have developed a process that I believe everyone should implement to be totally free from anger and resentment.

Wanting

The first step to forgive our enemies must be a strong desire to do so. Desire motivates us to do whatever we must do to achieve our goal.

I know we do not like to face this, but the reality is that we do what we like to do if our desire to do so is strong enough. "I cannot" usually means "I do not want to". None of us likes to take responsibility for the troubled areas of our lives. We definitely prefer to use excuses and guilt. But none of them will set us free. You have to want to forgive, and as soon as you do, the process will begin. Desire will come not by feeling but by conviction. You have to be convinced that unforgiveness will lead to total defeat. The desire to achieve victory and freedom must become the engine of your desire.

Deciding

After you really want to forgive, you must decide to do so. The decision cannot be emotional, it has to be what I call a "real decision". These kinds of decisions do not change when emotions change. It is a firm decision that is determined to make forgiveness a way of life.

This decision will not necessarily change the way you immediately feel, nor does it mean that you will not struggle with the idea of forgiving these people. Some people will need to forgive again and again, and many times because of what they did to you, that is definitely not an easy thing to do. It is something which must be done purposefully, without considering how we feel about it.

Depending

The next step in the forgiving process is to depend on God to help you do it. Deciding on your own is not enough. We need Divine Strength. Another one of the great victorious individuals in the Scriptures was the prophet Zechariah, who said that we would win our battles not by power or by force, but through the spirit. By connecting to the spirit, we will find Grace, which is the power to do what we need to do.

These processes are not easy. Forgiving my father was a long and painful process that prepared my character to keep me going through difficult times. I would need this process to be prepared for what was about to happen.

Things seemed to return to normal, little by little. Although we knew we had a trial without settlement, we tried to think or talk as little as possible about it.

It was already August 2009. The sun had not yet risen when my husband woke me up abruptly.

— *Something incredible just happened!* —he gasped.

—*I saw Jesus, he spoke to me, it was not a dream, I saw him in the room, he woke me up* — he kept repeating, stunned by what had just happened to him.

Applying the principle of Clarity:

I will activate the principle of clarity in my life by committing myself to take the next steps:

1. Today I will meditate on the unconditional love of God, and His patience with me.
2. I will write a list of those who have hurt me and who I have hurt and repeat the following prayer: *"Heavenly Father: I confess that I have not loved correctly, but that I am resentful of some people and I lack forgiveness in my heart".*

I regret this and ask you to forgive me.

I cry to you, Lord, to help me to forgive them completely.

Now I forgive: (Name them all, both living and dead) and I ask you, Lord, to forgive them also.

I accept myself and forgive myself for all my faults.

Amen".

5

The Principle of
CAUSE AND EFFECT

*H*ow come? — that was the first thing I thought of asking my husband while he insisted that he had seen Jesus in our room.

—I do not think it was a dream— he said again —. *I felt someone touched me on the shoulder to wake me up, and when I opened my eyes and looked to my left there He was, standing by my side of the bed. He was dressed in a radiant bluish white. I do not know how to explain it, but without saying anything, I knew with absolute certainty that it was Him. With his left hand, he showed me a white page with a circle drawn in the middle, and inside that circle a small figure, I understood that figure was me. On the paper, he showed me small arrows that moved from the edges of the paper to the center, but they bounced when they touched the circle, they could not enter where the small figure was. He then passed his right hand over the paper as if He were dusting it, and instantly the circle disappeared. Once again, I saw the small arrows that moved from the edges of the paper, but this time the circle did not have the circle so they entered the small figure and I heard him say: 'All these blessings will come to you when you change your postal code'.*

After a quick sigh, Dionny finished by saying:

—*My love, I feel we have to move out of Philadelphia.*

For a long time, both Dionny and I had felt that there was something special for us in Miami. We were constantly talking about how one day we would build our home there, but we had never dared to do it. We had it all in Philadelphia.

I do not know what to call my husband's experience, perhaps a dream that seemed real, maybe a visitation, a vision or an ecstasy. But something was certain, somehow God was sending us a message and we had to decide to act.

You and I are essentially infinite decision makers. In each moment of our lives we move in dimensions of limitless possibilities where we find access to an infinite number of decisions. Some of these decisions are made consciously and some unconsciously.

Each victorious individual has an arsenal of constant miracles that are indispensable to accelerate the manifestation of victory, therefore, the duration of the battle, its speediness or delay, will depend directly on the decisions you make every day, and the peace and happiness with which you live in the process. To deny the existence of miracles is to deny the existence of life itself. All miracles are the emanation of life and God is the giver of life. His voice will give you very specific directions. It will tell you everything you need to know. I have realized through my past experiences that the real question is not whether God speaks to us or not, the question is, are we listening? Making decisions based on fear prevents us from opening ourselves to the voice of the Spirit and thus, to the manifestation of marvelous miracles that take place during our battle.

The antithesis of fear is love. Miracles naturally occur as an expression of love. The real miracle is the love that inspires them. In this sense, everything that emanates from love is a miracle, while everything that emanates from fear is the opposite. This is the principle of Cause and Effect. Every action produces a reaction. What you harvest will depend on the kind of seed you sow.

In battle, for an effect to be a miracle, love must be the cause. That love comes from a decision and not from an emotion.

Love casts out fear

"I soon realized that day on the beach in Atlantic City, where we received the call that would start everything, was very important for our emotional stability and unity in the battle."

1 John 4:18

Nothing and everything cannot coexist. To believe in one is to deny the other. Fear is really nothing and love is everything. Whenever light penetrates the darkness, darkness is abolished.

The natural human reaction is to hide us during the battle creating a fictitious protection that in the end only inhibits miracles. Making decisions based on love means there is no fear of believing again and being exposed. They are conscious decisions, causes that inevitably translate into the effect of existence.

We decided to believe starting the day of the dream. We believed that God was somehow laying out a new horizon, and although we did not understand it we decided not to be afraid; hence, we began to look on the internet for a house to rent.

After a few days, we found a cozy apartment in North Miami Beach. Two months later we were driving a moving truck to that city. In the back of the truck was our car being pulled on a platform with wheels, inside the truck, our few belongings, and in the glove box, a letter from the Court that had just arrived to inform us that the final hearing would be January 10 of two thousand and ten, only two months later.

Although we still had to go through one more hearing, we made the decision not to imprison ourselves in the fear of uncertainty, but rather to pursue our dream. We understood that it is worse to make decisions with uncertainty and not with faith, because even if you like it or not, everything that is happening at this moment is the result of the decisions you have made in the past. Unfortunately, many of us make decisions unconsciously, and therefore we do not think they are decisions. And yet, they are.

We can choose to live in fear, or in love. In peace or despair, even during a battle.

If I insult you, you will surely make the decision to get offended. If I flatter you, you will surely make the decision to feel comfortable and appreciated. But think about this: it is still only a decision.

I can tell you offenses and insults, and you can still make the decision to not get offended. I can give you a compliment or say something beautiful and you can still make the decision to not feel flattered.

In other words, most of us, although we are beings of infinite decisions, have become a bundle of conditions and reactions constantly provoked by people and circumstances that produce predictable behaviors, or what is called "Pavlovian conditioning". Pavlov was famous for showing that if you give a dog something to eat every time a bell rings, very soon the dog will start salivating just by hearing the bell, because he has associated one stimulus with another.

Most of us, because of our conditioning, react predictably and reliably to the stimulus of our environment. Our reactions seem to be automatically provoked by both people and circumstances, and we forget that they are still decisions we just make, in every moment of our existence.

If you take a step back for a moment and witness the decisions you are making as you make them, then in this simple act of witnessing this you will change the entire process of an unconscious one to a conscious one.

The importance of the cause

Miracles are natural. When they do not happen, something has gone wrong.

When you make a decision, any decision, you can ask yourself two things: first, "What are the consequences of this decision I am making?" You will immediately know what they are in your spirit. Second: Will this decision that I am making now bring a spiritual purpose and happiness to me and those around me?

If the answer is yes, then go with that decision. If it is not, do not do it. It's that simple. The cause of your decisions will determine their effect. That is why the cause is important.

There will only be one decision outside of the infinite decisions we can make every second, which will bring real peace to us and to those around us, even in our battle. This is a miracle in itself. And that was exactly what my husband and I needed.

Making this decision without fear was like a new beginning, a new atmosphere, a new air. Fifty-two hours later I remember arriving at the small islands connected by bridges that seemed to be taken from a postcard. Finally, we were there. "Isle" (Normandy Isle) was the name of the island where we would live. A contemporary structure of whitened cement and large blue crystals stood imposingly before us. How couldn't we be excited? The building consisted of about five apartments of two floors each. After entering the parking lot next to the bay, we forgot what we were bringing. Our only mission at that moment was to enter through the doors and witness the interior of where we would live. It was indeed overwhelming, the first thing that captivated my eyes were the tall windows that served as a division between us and the sea. We really did not need to bring anything in, the place was fully furnished with the most beautiful furniture; the shades of creams and pale blue sprang around. Immediately I felt at home.

— *We will just use our room and desk set, the rest we will keep in a warehouse,* — I told Dionny as I walked my new place like a child in her imaginary castle. Two days later we had to travel to Panama to one of our conferences. I could not wait to be back to officially starting this new stage.

— *The desk is torn to pieces* — Dionny said as she opened one of the many boxes. We had already returned from Panama and anxiously placed our belongings.

— *Let's get a new one* —I answered. Excited, Dionny

looked for the nearest store, only to call me one hour later.

—*Did you find the store?* —I asked him when I answered my cellphone.

— *Better than that, I think I found the house that will be our home." I was driving back and as I passed the bridge I felt like driving around the island, I thought there might be a house for sale and there it was. It is not only by the sea, it is a foreclosure and it is possible that they sell it for much less than its original value.*

*—Even so, we do not have the money for that —*I said.

— Okay, but we have nothing to lose by asking.

Dionny wrote down the number and when we arrived, we called. One point one million dollars ended up being the price, which was definitely out of our budget. Without thinking about it, the night arrived and we went to bed.

— Again, you with your dreams — I said to Dionny joking, when he told me what he had dreamed about.

*— I was standing in front of the house —*Dionny went on—*. In the dream, I was surprised to see a vine, a plant full of grapes that stretched from inside the outer hallway that led to the sea, to the front gate. The vine had large leaves and pronounced vine shoots of green grapes. As I watched closely, the sky opened and I heard a voice say: You have access. Instantly the great gate opened and chains fell. What do you think the meaning is? —* Dionny concluded in puzzlement.

*—Well, if it has any meaning, I'd say it might be worth insisting. I'd like to see it —*I said.

We made the necessary calls and were given a code that would open the front door lock, giving us access to the property. The next day we were there.

The main entrance was to the left side of the house's front, where a solid steel gate inhibited entry to a covered hallway with a fountain that extended to two main doors and finally to the patio and the sea. We anxiously entered. The view was impressive. At the end of the bay you could see bayside and the big cruises departing towards the blue Caribbean Sea. We toured every corner but the biggest impression occurred at the exit.

As we talked about the dream and the vine that was supposed to be planted in the corridor and extending to cover the gate, we realized a detail that would change everything. Because of the darkness of the corridor the details of the steel gate were not visible from the outside, which changed drastically when viewed from inside. From the inside, the contrast between the outer light and the dark metal made us discover a detail that had been hidden for us. Surprisingly, as we looked at it from the darkness of the corridor we realized that the gate was formed by a vine of steel with large leaves and shoots of grapes. It could not be a coincidence. Would it be possible? Could it be another strange revelation?

With his hand extended softly Dionny touched the design of the vine and said:

—We do not have money to buy this house, but if this dream has been a revelation it means that we can somehow buy it. However, to be safe I will give a signal. If the price of one million one hundred thousand would lower to a PERFECT number, I do not know how, but God would provide the way to buy it.

I lifted my right hand and in a sign of affirmation I clapped it with my husband's.

Love and its effect

Darkness is the lack of light, just like fear is the lack of love.

When you are free from the fear of the battle your decisions are not based on the effect's uncertainty but on the cause's revelation. When you have been delivered from fear, your peace does not depend on the outcome of an uncertain future because doing so is based on control and control is no more than an illusion. Your peace depends on a present revelation that is not based on control but on faith.

The illusion of control leads you to a static state in the battle where your decisions do not work miracles but chaos, because everything causes you fear, and fear becomes the only cause.

Fear is not light, but darkness.

Escaping darkness involves two stages: first, recognizing that darkness cannot be hidden. This step usually leads to fear. Second, recognize that you can neither hide nor control anything even if you want to. This step makes you escape from fear. When you are willing to hide nothing, you will be willing to give the feeling of control toward the future and be free to experience peace and joy now.

During or after a battle, people who were injured usually pretend to hide behind an emotional armor for fear of being hurt again by people or future circumstances. I knew that for the three years we struggled with something that seemed to be interminable; but if fear of what would come next would have welcomed me, my decision would have been to reject everything that implied a new risk.

But deciding from love is different. God's love and His divine purpose is equivalent to the spontaneous effect of making the right decisions at the right time all the time, so all things work for good. It is this and only that revelation that produces great miracles.

It is the revelation that proves that God is constantly seeking ways to guide and draw our attention, but to act on it you must be willing to embrace the unknown.

That same afternoon we contacted a real estate agent named Mark Schoonover who helped us call the bank that was selling the house. After a long conversation, explaining the details of the house, Mark made a crazy proposal.

—*My client offers you six hundred thousand dollars in cash.*

Hearing him say that sounded so funny to me that I had to cover my mouth so as not to make noise. It was illogical and utterly ridiculous for my husband and I to get so much money, especially in cash, but I understand that Mark wanted to test how far the bank would get.

With a half-smile Mark hung up the cell phone and said:

— *Like I had predicted, the agent laughed in my face. He told me: 'impossible, the house is in foreclosure and the price has already been reduced to the minimum', but also said that if we paid in cash he can sell it to us in one million, but that he would have to consult it with his boss.*

—Well, you know the answer: impossible —
I replied. A few minutes later Mark called us to let us know that the boss had approved the one-million-dollar rebate, but we had already concluded that even as that, without credit it was impossible for us. That was it, well, that's what we thought.

—Unbelievable— was Mark's first expression when we answered his call—. *The bank just called me, they have made an impressive proposal.*

It was a Thursday, November 5, two thousand and nine. The days had passed and I had discarded the idea of buying that house. Dionny did not seem to understand what Mark was trying to explain, so he placed the call on speaker.
—President Obama has just approved a trillion dollar bailout for banks struggling with home foreclosures, and because it is from South Florida, this bank complies with the requirement, but there is one condition: only houses that are sold before the end of the year may apply, and the government would grant the bank the difference in real value of the house. But here comes the proposal: if you have the cash they are willing to sell you

the house for seven hundred and fifty thousand.

*—Is that all? —*Dionny asked.

*— Well, you must add the closing costs and other expenses, give me a minute —*Mark said while he was adding up the numbers.
— With all the expenses, you'd need exactly seven hundred seventy-seven thousand dollars in cash.
You can imagine Dionny's face when he heard the number. I was totally petrified. Seconds later, in a belated reaction, he looked at me and asked, *—How much? —*After Mark had repeated the number, I asked:
—How much do you need to sign the contract?
—Ten thousand dollars, but they would need to have the other seven hundred and sixty-seven thousand dollars by December the fourteenth, otherwise you will lose the down-payment.
*—We'll call you in a minute, —*Dionny said with a nervous voice.
*—My love —*Dionny whispered, touching my hand as he raised the volume of his voice. *—The signal that we asked for was fulfilled. Seven, perfect number. Seven hundred seventy-seven thousand, it is so exact that it sounds ridiculous. I do not know how we're going to do it, but God has given us this house.*
*—I believe so too—*I said.

We called Mark once more and asked him when we could sign the contract.

— *Tomorrow*—he said.

Indeed, from the little that we had managed to save over the years, we made a check for ten thousand dollars and the next day we were there.

Nervous, we signed each paper of the initial contract knowing that from that hour the clock began to tick. We had exactly one month and seven days to find the rest of the money, otherwise we would lose ten thousand dollars, and we had only fifty-eight thousand dollars left. For us it was an impossible task to achieve.

The following weeks were totally miraculous. The next day we traveled to Bogota to participate in a conference of Christian entrepreneurs organized by Alfredo Barrios, a pastor friend.

—*Dionny, I do not know you, but I feel something very strong in my heart.* — These were the words of Carlos Saez, an important Chilean entrepreneur, who we met during that activity. Without knowing anything about us and after introducing himself, he went on:

— *I've decided to help you, what's your most important project right now?*

— *Buy a house* — Dionny said with a smile.

— *How much do you need?*

You can imagine how nervous I was while I was listening in silence to the conversation. Dionny paused before answering the question:

—*Um... over half a million dollars.*

—*Okay* —the businessman continued calmly.

—*You have a hundred and fifty thousand from me.*

—*How come?* — Dionny asked, bewildered—. *A loan?*

There was another short silence but so intense that anyone could hear the beat of my heart. Finally, the businessman replied.

—*No, not a loan, a gift.*

Everything seemed so unreal, we had received gifts in the past, but never anything like this. But God was about to surprise us even more.

— From Puerto Rico, one of the most successful developers of marketing networks decided to *"bless us"* — were his words.

Others from Miami, Oregon, New York, Venezuela, Argentina did the same. The generosity was impressive, we had never experienced anything like it. And the strange thing is that they all used similar words, for no apparent reason they had been "moved to bless us," all this without having any idea of what we needed. The cause was having a miraculous effect.

It was already December fourteen of two thousand nine, it was the last day of the agreement, in only days, miraculously, and without asking for a cent, our account had increased ten times more. How not to believe in miracles? The blessings had been overwhelming ... but not enough.

Although we were stunned by everything that had happened, the final day had arrived and we still needed to complete the agreed amount. The worst thing was that Mark had told us that there was a counter proposal from another buyer offering far more money than us. In other words, if we did not comply with the contract at the appointed time, the bank would keep our ten thousand dollars and sell the house to the highest bidder.

It was midday and we knew that in only four hours we would lose the deposit and with it the house of our dreams.

Applying the principle of Cause and Effect:

I will activate the principle of cause and effect in my life by committing myself to taking the following steps:

1.   Today I decide to love without condition and without expecting anything in return. I will still love those who I believe do not deserve it.

2.   I will pray for a few minutes and because of love I will witness marvelous miracles.

3.   I will meditate on the things that caused me fear and I will refuse to try to control them by freeing myself from fear and accepting the complete freedom of the spirit.

The Principle
of
TRANSFORMATION

6

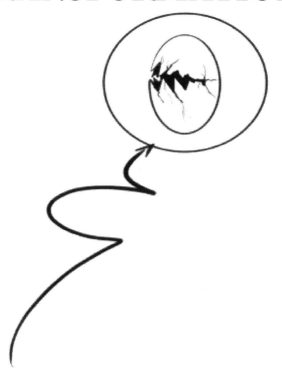

Minutes before two in the afternoon we received the most unexpected call. The Zamoras were a Mexican family that we had met on one of our trips to Guatemala. They lived in a small town called Nuevo Progreso, between the Mexican border and the Texas valley. In this unexpected call, the couple told us that for some days they had been trying to get in touch with us, since in their own words, "God had moved them to give us exactly eighty thousand dollars". The restlessness the couple said, had been so strong that they could not sleep the night before. What they did not know was that this was the exact amount we needed to be able to buy the house, not a penny more or a penny less. Amazing!

However, we still had a dilemma. It was already two o'clock in the afternoon and in two hours, the bank would be closed and with it, the opportunity. The big challenge was: How could they make an immediate transfer from Mexico? This kind of transfer takes about two days. If it were not possible, I could imagine how happy that bank would be to take our ten thousand dollars and sell this house at a higher price. How frustrating.

After telling them the situation and the reason for their restlessness, we were totally surprised:

—*You go to your bank, we will go to ours and see what can be done, this is definitely no coincidence.*

So, we did it. It took us forty-five minutes to get there. My heart wanted to get out of my chest, it was too much to assimilate in just thirty-eight days.

After explaining the situation, our banks got in touch. Only minutes before four o'clock in the afternoon. While the banks were looking for a way, we kept in touch over the phone with the family.

— *It's going to happen, this is no coincidence* — they said to keep the hopes up. But the truth was, it seemed that the effort was futile, there were only minutes left for the contract to expire.

—*Mr. Baez* — said the agent —. *The transfer was possible, you have complied with the contract. Congratulations, the house is yours.*

The miracle happened. Unquestionably, it was one of the happiest days of my life.

We were prepared to celebrate that New Year's Eve like we never had before. We would celebrate our last event in Caracas with a great friend, Raul Avila. The platform would be shared with great men of faith such as T.D. Jakes, Ronny Chavez, Aquiles Azar, Juan Ballistreri, Lucas Marquez and others. But one would define our lives, his name: Pablo Lay, a prominent prophet from Patagonia.

It was the fifth day of the conferences. Dionny and I were in the front row listening to the end of Ballistreri's presentation when Pablo approached us. With a deep look he took Dionny's right hand and in a very low voice said —*I see you're going to lead a church.*

—*How come... will I become a pastor?* —Dionny said, astonished. I knew that such a thing was the most remote among our plans, yet Pablo continued with his prophecy.

—*Yes, you will. And you will begin in the month of March; it will be very powerful, crowds will come from many places, craving for spiritual encouragement.*

—*And where will it be?* —I asked as if to test him.

—*I do not know, but I see palm trees by the side of the road before arriving at the place.*

Palm trees! I exclaimed within me. Although I did not say anything immediately, I visualized the millions of palm trees that were planted in Miami. Could he be more specific? This is ridiculous, I thought.

At that moment, he looked at me and said:

—*I know what you think, but I assure you these palm trees are different.*

Before he finished, Dionny interrupted him.

—*And how does the place look like?*

—*The walls are rustic and the color* ... —Pablo paused for a moment while looking for what to compare, and looking at one of the many wallets around said:

—*The color is like this* —referring to a mustard beige tone—. *Maybe a little lighter*— he said, leaving without saying anything else.

Dionny and I looked at each other, taken aback, even though we respected Pablo, I know we both had doubts about it. Wow, we had no idea at that time what we were about to go through.

The event ended and we returned to Miami ready to celebrate the end of the year with our relatives. There was much joy for our recent achievements, although deep inside we were a bit concerned due to what could happen during the final hearing.

The beginning of the end

As it is your desire, so it will be your intention. As your intention, your outlook. As your outlook, your action. And as your action, your destiny.

It was already two thousand and ten and the day was approaching. Dionny decided to travel to Sweden with Lucas Márquez to fulfill the first commitment of the year. Then he would return to Philadelphia on January 9, just one day before the final judgment. I waited for him impatiently, anxious because I knew that everything was about to end.

The long-awaited day had arrived. After what seemed like three endless years of legal Courts, long days and overwhelming challenges, everything was finally going to be defined this day.

Only a few minutes after nine in the morning we arrived at room 1103 of the Court of Philadelphia. Just before opening the majestic redwood door, I decided to squeeze my husband's right hand.

I wanted to reassure him that he was not alone and so it was, behind me was my mother, my two sisters, and my mother-in-law on the other side. All sure of an imminent victory.

— *Let's sit in the front* — I said —, *I want the Judge to see us until our turn comes* —I thought maybe the Judge would be pleased to see our openness.

Someone hit my left shoulder. It was Jamie who, after greeting us, said:

—*Do not worry, we've already won the first part of the case and I am pretty sure we'll win the final part today.*

— *What's the plan?* —Dionny asked.

— *You will wait here until our turn comes, then I will do all the talking, you will not say anything unless it's necessary.*

—*All stand, the Honorable Judge Harold Kane* —a voice exclaimed, as the private door opened and the Judge entered.

The trial officially took place. No more delays and postponements, this was the final moment. Although in my flesh I was living the extortion to which we were exposed to and for me it was obvious that we retained the truth...

I felt a certain fear. I felt uncertain because, due to all our recent occupations, the reality was that we had not prepared ourselves correctly for the trial.

The prosecutor was the first to present her argument. Jamie then went next, denying the allegations. Everything was so fast and absurd, a trial based only on word of mouth and without any tangible evidence.

The judge ordered a short recess.

Jamie took the opportunity to express his sole concern:
— *I'm just afraid the judge wants to cut the baby.*

—*What do you mean?*

— *I mean that like Solomon, the Judge may decide to try to stay well with both parties. Keep in mind that the first and worst part we won and what is left is insignificant, because it has no criminal repercussions.*

—*Insignificant to them* —Dionny snapped.

—*All rise* — the voice yelled, indicating that the recess had ended and the judge made his entrance to end the trial.

An intense silence filled the whole room until the Judge with two papers in his hand walked in, and fixing his glasses, he began:

— *In the case of Pennsylvania Common Welfare v. Dionny Baez, the criminal charge has been set aside.*

Immediately I took my husband's hand and took a deep breath as the judge went on:

— *As for the civil charge, Dionny Báez is declared...*

I squeezed both hands anxious to finish this nightmare.

—*Guilty* — said the Judge, dropping the hammer and with it, crushing our hopes. And now what? The prediction of our lawyer was fulfilled. The Judge had just cut the baby.

Transformation begins with the correct perception

"While we do not look at the things which are seen, but at the things which are not seen. For the things which are seen are temporary, but the things which are not seen are eternal".

(2 Corinthians 4:18)

At that very moment, we were paralyzed by a terrifying feeling, it was as if they had just locked us in a small room with all sorts of limitations, legal limitations, social limitations, and limitations of what people would say.

I know that so many other people have felt the same way as they go through their own battle, but by following that dangerous path, it is easy to end by limiting our destiny ourselves. At that moment, we did not really understand what could limit us, when we were everything. Consider this: look at the trees and your lungs. If the trees do not breathe, your lungs will not either. And if your lungs do not breathe, neither can the trees. The trees and your lungs are a single unified process. Winners understand that air is in their breath and that the energy of the sun and stars is also the energy that vitalizes their limbs and gives electricity to their brain.

This is a scientific fact. Your body is a dynamic interchange of all living bodies, including animals. We were created from the dust of the earth; therefore, I am in the universe and the universe is in me. We are all part of an interchange of coexistence that gives life to creation.
How can I believe that a situation can limit me?

How would I have liked to have understood this concept at that time. The identity of the winner is not based on "I am this" or "I am that" but in "I am everything in God" and "God is everything in me". The result is the ability to see the world as a master plan and to understand the true nature that surrounds us. This ability is an effective weapon against the fears produced by the judgment of others. Without it, we will always be limited to the conclusion that others have reached. Discovering it, the principle of transformation literally changes everything. We begin to be part of the instinctive and intuitive source of wisdom and power that has the ability to transform every day, every interaction and every moment into a creative experience.

Of course, the Judge's decision would produce in us what appeared to be a great limitation, but then I understood that in fact, every limitation is built up in the mind. Most of us look in the mirror and find the image of what we think we are. Perhaps, subconsciously we recognize that this image is only a compilation of what we are living or have lived, the judgment that others have placed upon us, past experiences both good and bad, and a projection of the person we believe to be. This reflection reinforces our self-image (our flesh), which often results in a continuation of harmful patterns of behavior and low self-esteem.

It is very tempting, in a situation like the one we were going through, to visualize ourselves as limited victims. And I think it was almost automatic because in reality, we did, until we realized that winners, however, see a different reflection. When they see themselves in the mirror they not only see their reflection but the mechanics behind it, which is very different. They not only see their past experiences, they also see their future. And they not only see their future, they also see yours and mine, that of their allies, their adversaries and all the others'. In Court, we did not understand everything, but we had to cling onto our faith that something transcendent would result in the end. It is a very difficult task, but not impossible. Failure to do so will lead you to believe that it is all over.

Winners have learned to live without these fictitious limitations between personal and universal. They have realized that everything has its purpose and everything in God ends up being part of something that transcends us.

When we live from the spirit, in the essence of our being, we not only find the ability to transform our situation; we have an obligation to do so.

It is in this way that artists see the world. They do not look at an object in the world and define it as independent from it. A basket of fruits, a stunning sunset, a wonderful statue. These things come to life through the artist's interaction with them. Artists bring them to life simply by perceiving them. This is the nature of everything that is created. When we realize that everything in our life exists because we interact with it, we gain a great sense of empowerment. Consequently, we receive the power to orchestrate what should be and what should not be in our life.

Especially as a woman, it is very easy to fall into the trap of feeling limited. One of the most impressive Biblical stories for me is that of Deborah, a great conqueror who, in times when women were heavily limited and downgraded by their culture, she was able to transcend these limiting obstacles and became a hero.

Deborah also had to face Judges. In fact, they ruled in Israel before the monarchy began. The Judges were charismatic leaders, selected by the people, and whose fundamental concern was that the roots that had allowed various nomadic groups to become a community should not be lost.

They had to face two problems: the hunger for power and wealth, and the neighboring farming and ranching peoples with whom the Israelites interacted. One of these neighboring villages that had the greatest influence was the Canaanite people.

The inferiority of women among the people of Israel was like that of other peoples and eras. Their testimony was not valid in court. Their word was not to be trusted. Over and above all the lower categories through which she might have been limited, Deborah excelled and triumphed. A victorious individual sitting under a palm tree resolved the complaints brought by the Israelites.

—*If you take with you ten thousand men of the tribe of Naphtali and fight against the Canaanite army, I assure you, you will have the victory* — were the words with which Deborah challenged Barak, commander of the Israelite troops.

—*If you go with me, then I will go*— said the commander.

Thus, a woman became a judge and prophet of the people of Israel, against all traditions, in a world where men assumed all social and religious responsibilities.

But the victory did not end there. As a judge, she dared to summon the tribes of Israel to wage war against Jabin the Canaanite king, and Sisera captain of his mighty army. Israel finds victory in the meager troops commanded by Deborah and Barak.

As a result, the country lived in peace for forty years.

Neither before nor after Deborah will you find in the history of Israel the case of another woman who was recognized for her authority. And her people did not go to her for advice, they went to stand for trial. Someone who could not even be a witness became a Judge. She exercised a leadership that will not be repeated in that nation by any woman throughout history.

Deborah, realizing the important role that each of us play in creation, sets us free. Otherwise, we will inevitably be trapped by the creation of our own limitations. Our actions and beliefs will be limited by our perspective. We will be convinced of our own inabilities, or that the world somehow has a plot to destroy us. No matter what the specific limitation is, the result is that without the transformation principle, we will be stuck, becoming fate's eternal victims.

In spiritual terms, transformation is not only to gain a new awareness of who we are, but also, the interpretation of events in a way geared toward a greater awareness, discerning the basic connectivity between all things. Transformation then becomes the ability to see and experience the world from an infinite number of perspectives. It is the ability to transform and then see the experience of the world not only from an individual point of view but from all other perspectives.

I heard someone once say, "Reality is an act of perception". When we become aware of that perception we take control of reality. What reality? That you are more than you think you are. The ability to change that perception, or point of view, is the art of transformation.

Transformation: from Flesh to Spirit

"There is therefore now no condemnation to those who are in Christ Jesus, who do not walk according to the flesh, but according to the Spirit".

Apostle Paul

—*Do not worry, everything will be fine, God is in control* —Dionny said, as the Judge was preparing to pronounce his verdict.

At that moment, it seemed impossible for me to see beyond the present, which was annihilating. I had to overcome my fears. What usually interferes with the process (after all, we were all born with it) is the flesh.

Our flesh is our self-image. It is not only the image of condemnation and judgment imposed by the world around us; it is the weakness with which we qualify and perceive ourselves when facing failure.

Let us go back to the mirror. Consider that reflection that looks at you. What you see is just a perception of what you think you are. So far, you can understand that even your supposed reflection is nothing more than a portrait of the biological dynamics occurring in your body. You are not only what you see, you are all those personal moments and memories from your history that have escalated into this present moment. You are also the hopes and dreams that motivate you to be what you want to be. But even this description does not do justice to who you really are, for it is only a self-image that you are looking at, and to define yourself according to your self-image results in a repetition of the same behavior patterns, repeatedly. Especially, if that reflection is not something that pleases you, the consequence is low self-esteem, and the perpetuation of a person in who you do not believe in. The only way to change this is by changing your perspective from your self-image, to your being.

Being is your spirit, who you really are, is connected with the highest values of truth and goodness. Free from borders that limit our own understanding of what God wants to do in our lives. Your spirit can see beyond the verdicts dictated by your situation, thus, creating a sense of purpose and hope, which is key to the victory in the battle.

It was not easy for us to learn this.

—*You are sentenced to four years of provisional supervision* —the Judge exclaimed, using the hammer once again.

— *I told you it was a very minor thing* — Jamie whispered, explaining that unlike regular probation, this did not require me to physically appear from time to time before the authorities. They just want to make sure that for four years you will not have any problems.

Although I felt at peace after hearing this explanation, I knew that the confrontation with the media in the coming days would be relentless.

At the end of it all, we entered a small office where the details of the process would be explained to my husband. During this time, a secretary with a very unwelcoming face was sitting down.

—*Fill in this form*—with a boring and not so

friendly tone, the lady grumbled from her small desk.

Dionny answered all the questions from the form.

Pulling out some small glasses from the desk, the lady was preparing to read it, she took the paper and her face changed immediately.

—*Miami?* — She asked after reading the address and continued—: *You know you're not going back to Miami, don't you?*

— *What do you mean?* —Dionny asked, surprised. I got up from a nearby chair where I was sitting and confused, I wanted to get a little closer.

—*It says here that the supervision will be done from Philadelphia and the person to be supervised must live in the same city.*

— *How is that possible?* — I thought. God would not allow such a thing. He moved us to Miami, supernaturally gave us a house we have not yet enjoyed. We had nothing in Philadelphia, we felt like visitors who needed to go home.

By now my hands were shaking. Nervous and anxious I could not resist the urge to interrupt.

—*But, madam, we have nowhere to live here, there must be a way.*

156

Angrily she replied:

—*You will have to request a transfer but it is a very long and complicated process. Your husband will be here for a long time.*

The verdict ended up being more serious than Jamie had explained.

— *Where are you staying?*

— *At my mother's*—Dionny said.

— *For now, you will have to make that your home*— the lady went on, checking and signing the papers—. *Write your mother's house address here, and all other instructions will be sent to you by mail.*

That way, we ended the most uncomfortable interview we ever had up until that point. You can imagine how confused we were.
What was the point of the dream and of the miracles that we have seen in the last months?

With a sense of defeat, we returned to my mother-in-law's house. It was the longest fifteen-minute trip of my life. Apparently, we had not yet learned some invaluable lessons from the past. If so, we would have realized that winners have no boundaries, nor limitations. That everything in the life of a victorious individual happens for a reason, and that if we listened carefully we would notice the 'whisper' behind each situation. If we had done so, instead of crying, we would have celebrated, as we would have realized that we were about to live the most beautiful time of our lives.

Applying the principle of Transformation:

I will activate the transformation principle in my life by committing myself to taking the following steps:

1. Today I will pray for a few minutes and meditate on the statements that have limited me. For example:

- I can't.

- I am a failure.

- Nobody loves me.

2. I will write a list of these statements and put them in a visible place to make sure they will never be spoken again.

3. I will meditate on the character of the Divine and before making any decision, I will ask what Jesus would have done about it, thus transforming me into who I truly am: A spiritual being.

Book Three

Dionny

No one learns anything unless they want to learn it and believe that somehow, they need it. It took me years of hard lessons to get to this last section.

It will be my mission in this final journey to show you that you already have the victory you are looking for, so you can understand that nothing real can be challenged, nothing unreal exists. In this, lies God's Peace.

The Principle of
SYNCHRONY

7

M iracles happen every day. Not only in distant villages or shrines on the other side of the world, they also occur here, in our own lives. They appear from their source, surround us with opportunities, and disappear again.

Although we think of them as extraordinary, the truth is that if we look carefully we will realize that we come across them every day. We may choose to acknowledge or ignore them, without realizing that our victory in battle may depend on it. The great conquerors of history recognized the presence of miracles, transforming their lives into an electrifying experience, more exciting than they had ever imagined. Ignore miracles and an opportunity will disappear forever.

Beyond your physical body there is a spiritual world where, connected with God, everything is possible; even miracles. Especially miracles. That part of you is intertwined with all that exists, and even that which does not exist yet.

We have all experienced events that may be considered to be inexplicable or astounding. Maybe you were cleaning your closet and found a gift from someone who you had not talked to for years; then, an hour later, out of nowhere, that same person calls you on the phone. Or maybe you were injured with your car on a lonely road, and when you were about to give up, the first car to appear is a tow truck.

Can these types of events be described as mere coincidence? Of course, but when they are examined more closely, they can also be seen as miraculous flashes in our lives.

I do not believe in coincidences without meaning. I think every coincidence is a message, a clue about some facet of our lives that requires our attention.

When you live your life in appreciation of coincidences and their meanings, you will begin to understand that God, in His infinite wisdom, is connecting you with a purpose so great that it goes beyond you. It is here where miracles happen. I call it the state of synchrony.

Synchronicity requires connecting to your creator and gaining access to a deep place within yourself, while at the same time you awaken to a gala of coincidences in the physical world. It requires understanding the deep nature of things, recognizing

God's infinite wisdom while you are willing to pursue divine opportunities as they appear.

The supernatural will be a constant in your life when you learn to perceive it and appreciate its nature. I think that has been my case.

It was May of two thousand and ten, once again, abruptly, I woke Yari up, impressed and eager to tell her what had just happened. This time we were sleeping in a small room in my mother's house.

For months, we had struggled against the system to be able to move back home but with no success. In contrast, our violent sense of injustice and insatiable insistence had created a growing friction between the judge and us. Our last resort was to submit our case to the Supreme Court of Justice hoping that in some way they would honor its name. The problem was that we would have to wait indefinitely to know whether the Court would decide to take the case or not, without any assurance that their decision would be in our favor. We could not leave the city without asking for permission. We almost gave up, we did not have any other option but to lose our privacy and live in that little room in my mother's house, but we held onto the hope that we would soon return to our home.

It had to be about six o'clock in the morning. The faint rays of the sun seeped through the thin curtain. It was one of the three small rooms on the second floor of the house. My mother slept in the first one, there was a small office in the second, and we stayed in the third. As we entered the room we stumbled upon a 'single' bed, the smallest of its kind, glued to the right wall of the small hallway. The wall on the left had a window that faced an alley. Although it was a little tight, we had already become accustomed to this space. The night before seemed to be just like any other night, like many others before it, nothing super spiritual or mystical. I remember that the World Cup was about to start and we had gone to bed late after watching a replay of a match. Maybe we were so tired, we forgot to pray that night. Nothing would indicate what was about to happen.

As the morning brought light into the room, I remember being half-asleep. Yari slept on the bedside toward the wall, I, on the bedside toward the hall.

Have you ever felt like someone is watching you? Then you will know exactly what I felt. It was as if someone had entered the room. As I instinctively opened my eyes I saw a man was there, by my bed. You can imagine my reaction, 'a thief' was the first

168

thing I thought. Scared, and looking for something to hit him with, I heard a voice that said to me: "he is a prophet".

I had never had an experience like this, nor can I explain what it meant, how can a prophet be in my room? I do not know, I can only retell what I went through. It was not a dream, he was standing next to my bed, he was tall, had semi-dark skin, looked strong and had a beard, I would say he looked around forty. Immediately with his right hand he grabbed his head and began to move back and forth as he stood in the same spot... And finally, he spoke.

— *One hundred. October one hundred* — and kept repeating it until for some reason I interrupted.

— *In October, a hundred times more* —I said.

— *That's it* — he said —. *God will give you a hundred times more in October.*

When he finished saying those words, he vanished.

When I woke Yari up and told her what had happened, she suggested that we began fasting in October, eating nothing until six o'clock in the afternoon and repeating it for the rest of the month.

—*Alright!* —I said excitedly. I was sure that in October, God would bring justice on everything they had done to us. In some way

I would get out of this legal problem.

— *But how about we pray all month too*— Yari added—. *What's more, we can talk to the owner of the radio to allow us to pray every day of the morning fast in his sanctuary...*

Instantly the direction of her gaze shifted, she paused, and slowly raising her right hand as if to hide something, she ended up saying, —*Wow, I see it, imagine that we can do a miracle service every week, we could do it on the Friday nights of our fast... we would call it 'Friday of Glory'.*

Indeed, the city radio station had a small sanctuary in the middle of the building, which was only used on Tuesday mornings. This was the same radio station where the announcer had spoken about me, and that director was the same one I met years earlier, the same one that had suggested the lawsuit to me. It would be absurd to present him with an idea like this after all we had gone through. I did not know that synchrony was already in action.

Synchrony and coincidences

What you call coincidence is nothing more than the miraculous arrangement of the events that will define your destiny.

Sarrail had worked for over twenty years at the radio station he founded. He was a controversial man, with great passion and respect within the city. Yari's idea was great, but there were two problems. First of all, how to call him after so long without communicating? And second, how to present such an abrupt idea? Discouraged, I decided to wait. My surprise was great, when that same day I received a call. Yes, that same day.

—Dionny, long time no see. I heard you have been in the city for a few months, would you like it if we meet?

I could not believe it, it was Sarrail, how could such an immense coincidence happen? God was synchronizing something.

Victorious individuals have understood the importance of synchronized events during the battle, which seem like mere coincidences.

Talking about coincidences as coded messages sent from the spirit world sounds like a mystery novel, but it's real. Pay attention, look for the clues, decipher their meanings and eventually the truth will be revealed. In many ways that is exactly what happens. In the end, life is a mystery.

What makes life a mystery is that our destiny seems to be hidden from us, and it is only when we end our lives that we find ourselves in the position of looking back and seeing the paths that we followed. In retrospect, the narrative of our lives seems perfectly logical. We can easily follow the threads of continuity that have shaped our life experiences. Even now, wherever you are in your life, you can look back and notice how naturally your life has flowed from one stage to the next. Imagine how easy it would have been if you had only known where the road led you. Some look back and wonder, why was I so worried? Why was I so hard on my children, or on myself?

If we only learned to live from the level of the spirit all the time, we would easily appreciate the great truths of life. We would know them beforehand. The road would be clearly discernable and we would not need clues, or signals, or coincidences.

However, most of us do not live from the spiritual level all the time, so we depend on what we call coincidences to get a better idea on how to become winners in the battles of our journey.

We have all had coincidences in our lives. The word itself perfectly defines its meaning: "co" means "with", and "incidence" means "event". Hence, the word coincidence refers to events or incidents that occur simultaneously with other incidents. One or more events occurring at the same time. And because an experience of a coincidence is universal, most people underestimate it. Little strange events of life in which we marvel but quickly forget.

Coincidences are more than just entertainment. When you begin to see life's coincidences as opportunities, every coincidence becomes meaningful. Each match becomes an opportunity to take advantage in the battle. Every coincidence becomes the opportunity for you to be the winner that God has destined you to be.

This is the ultimate truth of synchrony, that God himself is conspiring from the spiritual realm to help you achieve your victory. To do this God uses "acausal connections".

Acausal connections

And we know that all things work together for good to those who love God, to those who are the called according to His purpose.

Apostle Paul

What is an acausal connection? If we analyzed deeply the incidents of our lives we would realize that we all have a history interwoven with our personal destiny. Acausal means that the incidents are connected to each other but have no direct cause-and-effect relationship, at least superficially. They are acausal, from the Latin word "without cause".

We cannot even imagine the complexity of the forces behind each event that occurs in our lives. The only reason we do not experience synchrony in our lives is because we do not live on the level where it occurs.

The reality is that what you see is not the true reality. True reality is behind the curtain. Really, we are not here. This is our shadow. What we experience as everyday realities is a mere projection of what is actually happening in the spiritual realm. Behind the curtain is a soul, living, dynamic and immortal, beyond the reach of time and space. Acting from that level we can consciously influence the outcome of our battles. In synchrony, we participate consciously in the creation of our lives by understanding and believing that there is a spiritual world much more powerful than where we live. Sarrail's call could be taken as a mere coincidence, but in reality, it involved much more than that.

— *Sure, I can see you tomorrow if you wish.*
— I replied to Sarrail, still dumbfounded by his unexpected call.

And I was there a day later. I had no idea why he wanted to get together with me, but I was sure of something: it was the perfect opportunity to present him our idea.

After a few minutes of waiting, I walked slowly into the office. After a handshake, a hug and a few minutes of protocol questions (how are you?... how is your family?... etc.) it was time to know what the reason was for such a coincidence of a call.

— *Are you living in Philadelphia?* — Sarrail asked as if he were to address the reason for his call.

— *Yes, for a few months now* — I said as I sat down on a small chair in front of his desk.

— *Are you traveling a lot?* —he continued.

—*Not as much as before. Why? Do you have something in mind?*

As I asked him, something made me feel that I was going to have a good chance to make my proposal after hearing what he had to say to me. What he answered really shocked me.

— *Well, you see, for some time I've been talking to Izquierdo, my programming director, to have a prayer time program in the mornings, but we have never been able to do it. I do not know how busy you are, but when I found out that you were back in the city I thought maybe you could. Moreover, I had even thought of adding these prayers to a night of miracles, but I know that you travel on weekends.*

—*When do you want to do this?* — I asked, although I was very sure inside of how he would respond. Of course, it would really have to be something if he were to say to me: "On Fridays" ...

That was exactly his response.

—*What's more, I have the name* —he added—. *Fridays of Glory.*

It was the straw that broke the camel's back. I did not know what to say. I moved in slow motion and had an impressed face and took out my cell phone.

—*Okay, if I tell you, you will not believe me,* —I said—. *So, I'm going to put my wife on the speaker so you can hear what she's going to say.*

Yari was quick to answer. —*Honey, I have you on speaker phone, Sarrail is listening. I want you to tell him what we talked about yesterday.*

—*About the prayers?* —she asked.

—*Yes, tell him.*

—*Well, was it about praying every morning in the sanctuary?* —Yari asked, unsure of what we wanted to hear.

—*Yes. And tell him what else we wanted to do.*

—*Nights of miracles?* —she inquired.

By now Sarrail's face began to change, he could not believe what he was hearing. But the most impressive thing was about to happen.

I asked my last question: —*Tell him when -*

we wanted to do it and how we planned to call it.

Without thinking for more than second, Yari replied:
—*Fridays of Glory, because it would be Friday night"*.

I have tried to be as exact as I possibly can while recounting the story of what happened. Although impressive, those who were involved in this synchrony of it all know that every word is true.

Sarrail did not need to hear any more. He got up from his chair with his hand on his head, took a few steps to the left of his desk, and looking at me said—*We have to start doing this now.*

This happened on a Tuesday. That same week the commercials were already on the air to promote the prayers or "intercessions", and the nights of miracles. On Monday we began our daily inter-actions at seven o'clock in the morning, which we called "beginning your day with God", and eleven days later we began our first "Friday of Glory".

Attention and Intention

It is the Spirit who gives life; the flesh profits nothing. The words that I speak to you are spirit, and they are life.

Jesus

Your spirit will orchestrate your activity in response to two things: Attention and Intention. That thing to which you place your attention will flourish. The one which you take your attention from, withers. Winners are constantly watching out for any unusual event, no matter how big or small. They understand that they can be messages of the spirit carrying some necessary clue to the synchrony of events that will lead them to victory.

In the Bible, you will find victorious individuals like Mordecai, who understood that it was more than a coincidence that Esther, being Jewish, would have been chosen as the Queen of Persia at the exact moment when they planned the genocide of the Jews. However, he understood that Attention, although powerful, cannot work alone, an intention is necessary to manifest the purpose of the events synchronized by the spirit. That is why he says to Esther: *"For if you remain completely silent at this time, relief and deliverance will arise for the Jews from another place, but you and your father's house will perish. Yet who knows whether you have come to the kingdom for such a time as this?"* (Esther 4:14).

Winners like Abraham, who did not see as a mere coincidence that a ram that was entangled in a bush a second after God told him not to sacrifice his son. (Genesis 22:13).

Or Jonah, vomited by a large fish, was exactly on the island where God asked him to be. (Jonah 2:10).

Every event of synchrony is introduced by what we might call coincidence, but it is not until we bring attention and intention, that we will see it manifest itself.

Intention is not necessarily desire. Desire alone is weak because it is completely linked to the result that is longed for. Intention is desire without strict attachment to a particular result. It is the winner who acts on what he has perceived in the spirit, which is more important than the desired result.

Your intention is then for the future manifestation of an eternal purpose far from any selfish desire. Your attention is for the present. As long as your attention is in the present, then your intention for the future will manifest, because the future is created in the present. Accept the present and intend the future. The future is something that can always be created, but you should never fight against the present.

Do not wish to give up due to what you are living in the present, or what you have lived in the past. Past, present and future are all properties of consciousness. The past is a recollection, memory; the future is anticipation; the present is attention. Both the past and the future only live in the imagination. Only the present is real. He who is intent on the past or the future lives a fictitious life. But the one who pays attention to the present and intentions based on what he or she perceives from the spirit for the future will synchronize a multitude of events that will lead him or her to victory. This synchronization of events is possible since in the end, everything is connected with everything else. In nature, we see this clearly. Moles get outside of the ground and we know that it is already spring. Birds migrate to a certain direction at some time during the year. Nature is a symphony. And the symphony is being silently orchestrated from the foundations of creation.

The human body is another good example of this synchrony. A single cell in the human body makes about six trillion things per second, and you must know what each of the other cells is doing all the time. In the same way, everything is directly or indirectly connected. In the spiritual world, these connections are visible. But in the physical world we only see flashes of those connections through the clues that coincidences give us.

Attention and intention become powerful weapons for a victorious individual, because what you focus on not only gives you life, but also attracts you.

Therefore, the more attention you place on coincidences, the more you will attract other coincidences that will help you better understand the strategies you should aim for in your battle. It is the formula of a sure victory.

Even if you do not always understand the reasons, you must seek to fulfill the intention of the spirit. In due time, you will realize that things were not necessarily as you perceived them.

We started doing Fridays of Glory in October, the Miracles were awesome. People from many countries began to visit us to be participants of what was happening. It was beautiful, but we had a problem: we were not seeing what we really wanted; the reason for our prayers; of our fasting.

Days passed; October ended... then November, December, we were still fasting all those months. However, there was no response from the Court. Maybe that character that appeared in my room mentioning "October" was wrong?

Applying the principle of Synchrony:

I will activate the principle of synchrony in my life by committing myself to taking the following steps:

1. Today I will pray for a few minutes and meditate on how what I have called coincidences in my life have played an important role in my destiny until today.

2. I commit myself to being attentive to what I perceive as coincidences around me, and with each success, I will ask the spirit how to take the opportunity from them.

The Principle of
TRANSCENDENCE

8

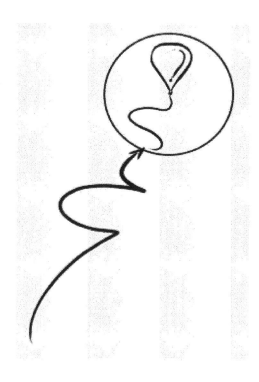

T*oday we are going to celebrate our first Friday of Glory*— Yari said excitedly.

It was October fifteenth of two thousand and ten. We had made all the preparations to begin our first night of miracles.

People had come from many places. The event began at seven in the evening and by six-thirty the place was completely full. Cancer patients, paralytics, blind, sore, vicious, sick, and healthy people, had come together to experience some miraculous move in their lives. Yari and I were no exception.

The night started and I immediately realized that something inside of me had changed, somehow it was not the same. I took the microphone for the first prayer, passionately asking Jesus to heal the oppressed and to touch all those present, but something had happened inside me, it was as if I felt what the people I prayed for were feeling.

Silvia Bautista was the first miracle of the night. When I approached this unknown woman, I felt a strong pain in my left pectoral.

Immediately I dared to declare through the microphone what I thought she had.

— *There are two cancerous tumors on your left breast and you have not told anyone, not even your husband.*

Instantly she began to cry, she could not explain how I knew. The truth is, I could not explain it either. In fact, she affirmed that after a recent medical study she had been diagnosed this mortal condition. Afraid and not wanting to worry her loved ones, she had not shared it with anyone. How impressive for all of us: during the prayer the tumors had disappeared completely. A few days later, she visited her doctor, who was astonished to confirm this healing. Silvia was free of cancer.

This was only the first miracle of thousands to follow. For four years, Maria suffered from AIDS, after new medical studies she was declared healthy. Argengy Ventura needed a kidney transplant, the doctors did not explain what had happened, after prayer his kidney was like new. Carmen Rodriguez was healed of a terrible disease in her muscles and walked after being two years and some months in a wheelchair.

The news of what was happening began to spread like fire. People began traveling from many countries to participate in what was happening.

Chile, Argentina, Venezuela, Honduras, Colombia, Mexico, among many others; Countries that we could not visit came to us. The city we looked upon with reproach, the territory of our defeat and frustration, became our delight. The principle of transcendence had been activated.

Transcendence is the most fundamental basis of a winner's nature. The ability to access transcendence is the last step toward knowing yourself and reaching your full potential. Through this ability, victorious individuals can go deep inside, beyond the secret passages and mental attics full of skeletons, into the very essence of being. Winners do not need to look at the world, see its chaos and hide from it. Rather, with the principle of transcendence, winners confront chaos and understand that they are both citizens of chaos and masters of it.

To reach this transcendence, winners have had to awaken to the true reality of the universe. In this reality they have realized that, finally, our battle is not against anything other than ourselves; they have understood that conflicts even against their worst and biggest enemies are truly, internal conflicts.

When you conquer those internal conflicts no one can defeat you, because you have reached a level that defeat itself cannot reach. From this level, the supernatural is natural.

During the process, I realized that each battle is indispensable. God himself is in charge of exposing ourselves to elements that we perceive as opposites in order to awaken us to His divine nature.

Each of us carries the potential of extraordinary miracles, but it is not until we face ourselves, and we conquer challenges, that we realize it. Everything that was happening every Friday night was not abnormal. Today I understand how abnormal it is to live from a reality where miracles do not happen and defeat is imminent.

The Reality of Realities

"My concern is not whether God is on our side; my greatest concern is to be on God's side, for God is always right."

Abraham Lincoln

You will realize that there are three different levels of realities.

The first level is the reality of matter, where objects and the physical world exist. Every day this reality is composed of objects existing in time and space. These objects are material, temporal and ephemeral. They are subject to decomposition, they experience the flow of linear time and are rigidly linked to cause and effect relationships. These objects are continually observed by conscious beings who have physical bodies. Many of these sentient beings fall into the error of believing that this is the highest level of reality, when in truth, it is only the product of intangible realities. Living from this reality leads you to be a prisoner of physical chaos, constantly failing. At this level lie disease and decline. It is impossible to be victorious from it.

The second level is the reality of consciousness, where emotions, feelings and thoughts exist. At this level, the soul lies, or what many call, the heart. It is a dangerous level of reality in which many are trapped by their emotions and cannot escape, becoming individuals, whose decisions and actions are based on feelings; "soul" people. In his book, the prophet Jeremiah refers to being guided by the emotions of the soul in this manner:

"The heart is deceitful above all things, and desperately wicked; who can know it?"
Jeremiah 17:9-10.

The third level of reality is above the reality of objects or consciousness. This is the most important and is the source of all existence. This is the reality of being, where the spirit exists. Being is a field of transcendence. Transcendence means not existing in time and space, therefore, being eternal. The spirit has no beginning in time, has no end in time and has no boundaries in space. In the same way that DNA differentiates my eyes from my nose, hair, skin, liver and all the wonderful parts of my body. In the same way, the spirit also differentiates the parts that create our total reality.

Victorious individuals understand that material reality is only an illusion, as it is a projection of the deepest levels. And that the reality of consciousness will lead you to live in emotional prisons if it is not deeply governed by the spirit, the being, who lastly is connected to the spirit of God. This is the principle of transcendence.

During one of the most difficult moments for the Apostle Paul, who is one of my favorite winners, he said: *"I can do all things through Christ who strengthens me."* He also said: *"it is no longer I who live, but Christ lives in me."* For Paul, Christ was more than a person, He was a state of being, an inner revelation. The Christ within you will awaken the state of the Son of God, where nothing is impossible, where miracles are normal and Victory is imminent.

The nature of Christ gives us access to the benefits of the Kingdom of God, which we have already understood is not a distant place beyond the stratosphere, but an accessible dimension among us, where God's purpose or will is manifested; Your Kingdom come, your will be done. This was the revelation that led Apostle Peter to receive the keys of the Kingdom when Jesus asked his disciples: *"But who do you say that I am?"*

—*You are the Christ, the Son of the living God* — said Simon Peter.

—*Blessed are you, Simon Bar-Jonah* —said Jesus—, *for flesh and blood has not revealed this to you, but My Father who is in heaven... And I will give you the keys of the kingdom of heaven, and whatever you bind on earth will be bound in heaven, and whatever you loose on earth will be loosed in heaven.*

That was exactly what was happening every Friday. What I stated was manifest, because I did not state it; in essence, my nature had changed.

Peter knew that it was one thing to know Jesus, the physical person, but another to know the Christ.

Christ cannot be known from the material reality, which is why Jesus responds: "*flesh and blood has not revealed this to you* (the material realm)*, but My Father who is in heaven* (God in the spiritual realm)".

Paul demonstrates that Christ is a state of being. In it, through Jesus' sacrifice, God's purpose is manifested, awakening within you who you really are.

This level of reality is immeasurable, it is all that was, all that is, and all that is to come. Winners know this state of infinite possibilities, recognize it as their true identity, and can access it at any time, in any place and in any circumstance.

Winners do this by accepting, without anxiety, that for those who live from that state of being wake up to the eternal purpose they were created for.

Let us briefly review the following text written by Paul to the Roman church, chapter 8:29:

For whom He (God) foreknew, He also predestined to be conformed to the image of His Son, that He might be the firstborn among many brethren.

Moreover, whom He predestined, these He also called; whom He called, these He also justified; and whom He justified, these He also glorified.

What then shall we say to these things? If God is for us, who can be against us?

He who did not spare His Own Son, but delivered Him up for us all, how shall He not with Him also freely give us all things?

Paul says that God did five things for us from the reality of the spirit:

1. He met us. Therefore, since God is spirit, each of us are also spirits and are connected for eternity, even long before we were born. If He knew us, we also knew Him, that denotes all wisdom and intelligence. Then, the wisdom of the universe lives within us.

2. He predestined us. We were sent to the earth with a purpose, a specific predetermined destination. When you consider the infinite improbability of circumstances, synchronies, miracles, and immense events that have had to occur to generate this moment, your existence in it, and all relationships, experiences and interactions that make you who you are, you will start to understand transcendence.

You are the product and culmination of every event that has brought you up to this moment; God has conspired in every episode of your life to bring you here. Although this is a very overwhelming thought, yet it affirms the reality that your existence is an extension of the universe into the vast, eternal, and minutely calculated purpose of God. If some period before this had been different, however minor, you would not exist in the same way that you exist today. When you awaken to the reality of the spirit, your steps are guided to the place of your assignment and the conquest of your destiny.

3. He called us. Throughout history naming something or someone denotes a sense of belonging. You only name what belongs to you. Paul says that God called us, gave us a name, you belong to him, you are his son, and the good news is that God will never leave what belongs to him in defeat.

4. He justified us. From that state of being, nothing and nobody can condemn you. To reaffirm this principle Paul writes to the

Roman church: *"There is therefore now no condemnation to those who are in Christ Jesus, who do not walk according to the flesh, but according to the Spirit"*. From this state, you transcend condemnation and guilt, two of the chief causes due to which battles are fought.

5. He glorified us. Only the one who conquers is glorified. God himself secures the victory those who transcend their spiritual being. The most interesting thing is that Paul teaches that God did all this with us before we were born.

He or she who is able to transcend has embraced each of these concepts, therefore he or she is sure that nothing that can happen, even those things that seem catastrophic, will work for evil.

Your spirit is not a thing. It is the potential of all things. The nature of your spirit is omniscient. Not omniscient in the sense of having information stored as Wikipedia, it is rather intuitive. It is the source of intuition, the source of intention, the source of imagination, the source of creativity, meaning, purpose and decision-making.

From conscious to transcendent

"I cannot be awake for nothing looks to me as it did before, or else I am awake for the first time, and all before has been a mean sleep".

Walt Whitman

How to forget that cold December day, only two months had passed since we started Fridays of Glory. Although we were living during a time of supernatural things we experienced every week, even though we had the opportunity to do what we were most passionate about in our city and see the crowds traveling from so many places, even though so many things had turned in our favor, there was still a detail, a huge detail that frustrated us. By the determination of the Court we remained deprived of the opportunity to travel, and worse, in front of so many thousands, we appeared guilty. The happiness of the achievements was at times tainted by the horrible internal frustration of not having overcome the judge, but then we were appeased by the remote possibility that the Supreme Court would take our case and perhaps... just maybe, justice would be done.

A rustle of hurried footsteps echoed from the wooden staircase. It was Yari, desperate to reach the room where I was. When I opened the door I remember seeing her intrigued face and a letter in her right hand.

—*A letter from the Supreme Court has just arrived.*
—Nervously, she jumped sporadically as she spoke.
— *Will today be the day of our final victory?*
—She finished saying as a statement of faith and as waiting for my approval to open the letter.

I must admit that my heart froze once more. What I was about to read would be key to what was to happen.

I firmly believe that God Himself moved the tokens in each episode to bring us to the revelation of the principle of transcendence. But he does so not only with Yarissette and with me, he does so with each one of those who make up his creation. God will do what is necessary to awaken you to this reality. The reality that you were not only fully created, but that you were created perfect.

The ability to overcome is a fundamental aspect of God, which he gave to his son. During creation, God extended himself to the created man and infused him with the same loving will that He possesses. There is no defeat in you. Because of the resemblance you keep with your Creator you are naturally a winner. No child of God can lose that faculty, for it is inherent in what he or she is. In essence, God created His children to be an extension of all that He is. This extension takes place when our awareness awakens. The improper use of the extension-the projection-takes place when you believe that there is some lack or defeat in you, and that you can supply it with your own ideas rather than with the truth. This process comprises the following steps:

First: you believe that your mind can change what God created.

Second: you believe that what is perfect may become imperfect or deficient.

Third: you believe that you can distort the creation of God, including yourself.

Fourth: you believe that you can be your own creator and that you are in charge of the direction of your own creation.

These distortions, related to each other, are a faithful reflection of what actually happened in the separation or deviation towards sin. None of this existed before the separation, nor does it really exist now. Everything that God created is similar to Him. The extension, as God created it, is similar to the inner radiance that the father's children have inherited from Him. His true source is inside but was disconnected at the time of separation.

The garden of Eden - the condition that existed before separation - was a state of being in which nothing was needed. When Adam heard the "lies of the serpent", all he heard was falsehoods. You do not have to continue to believe what is not true unless you choose it. All of it can disappear in the twinkling of an eye because it is nothing more than a false perception, a dream. What you see in dreams seems very real. Moreover, the Bible mentions that Adam fell into a deep sleep, but no reference is made anywhere that he was awakened from it.

To transcend this is necessary to wake up. We awaken when we accept the atonement of the Son of God, which allows you to realize that your defeat never actually occurred. For that, the Son was surrendered, to reconnect our spirit and to awaken us to the true reality.

Human beings are souls that possess a spirit and live in a body. The Bible teaches that the soul is a living soul, but only the spirit is life-giving. In other words, the soul has levels of consciousness, that is why it is alive, but it is only when we awaken the spirit that we pass from alive to giving life, from living to life-giving.

I would say there are four states of consciousness of the soul:

Sleeping conscience. Even when we sleep we may have some state of consciousness. For example, if, while you are asleep, you hear someone yell, "your house is burning", you would get up and run, because even when asleep you are still conscious.

Awaken conscience. This is when we awaken from physical sleep. However, if you live your hours awake without realizing what is inside you, then you are really dreaming awake.

Spiritual conscience. This state of consciousness alerts us to the fact that the past states of consciousness are only the result of the spiritual. In this state people are aware that there is a spiritual world, which is the source of benignity and evil, victory and defeat, life and death, darkness and light, salvation and perdition. However, they do not necessarily know how to live from the right source, they have only perceived that it exists. Most are wandering in this state, aware that there is something beyond, but they do not know how to reach it. They know God exists, but they do not know how to reach Him. Even worse, in this state, many surrender to darkness, hoping to achieve some victory by worshiping things that are not correct.

Divine conscience. This is where transcendence happens. It is when our soul connects to the Spirit and lives from it through God's atonement, becoming a life-giving spirit. There we find our true identity as children of God and activate all His nature in us. In this state there is no fear, because fear is only an illusion, in essence, it is not real. In this state, only truth lives, therefore everything unreal vanishes, giving space only to light and what emanates from it. Sin and guilt are darkness, why waste time fighting sin or guilt? When all darkness is exposed to light it cannot subsist, without effort it disappears. That is why "he who is born of God does not sin because he does not know sin", from this state it is impossible to live in fear, anxiety, or guilt. Light fills everything.

Guilt is the root of failure, of defeat; he who has no guilt has no defeat, therefore he lives without fear. Transcendence is what makes you more than a winner. It is to be aware that neither death, nor life, nor angels, nor principles, nor present, nor to come, nor anything created, there is no situation that can separate us from the love of God. That is the perfect love that casts out fear, and if there is no fear there is no doubt, therefore you live in a state of being in which all things are possible, all miracles, all victories. When you have transcended, what you formerly saw as loss now you see it as gain. What was defeat for you, you now understand to be part of a purpose and you see that victory is imminent. From this state, it is impossible to lose.

Nervously we opened the letter. What will be the news? Finally, light at the end of the tunnel?

There were many written words, but they were all summed up in the initial opening of the letter:

""Mr. Dionny Baez, we hereby inform you that your request to reopen your case through the Supreme Court has been denied." Apparently, our legal battle was not important enough to be reviewed by the Supreme Court. And now that?

We were on the verge of winning, and we did not know it. The way we would win would exceed our expectations. The principle of transcendence had been activated.

Applying the principle of Transcendence:

I will activate the principle of transcendence in my life by committing myself to taking the following steps:

1. Today I decide not to judge people or situations. I will observe things as they are and pray for wisdom to transform them. I will observe things as they are and pray for wisdom to transform them.

2. I reject my past nature and accept the nature of the spirit. I reject my past nature and accept the nature of the spirit, from now my mind is linked to Christ, my DNA is God's DNA, and therefore it is impossible for me to lose.

3. Victory is part of my new nature, I will accept it always, even if it seems like the opposite.

9

The Principle of
MANIFESTATION

W*hy did they choose those horrible palm trees?* —I was telling Yari while we were driving to celebrate another Friday of Glory. Apparently, one of the city's politicians thought it was a good idea to install a pile of metallic gray palm trees on the edge of 5th Street, which is on the way to the Church. Though it was barely four o'clock in the evening, it seemed like night time, the noise of the crowds on the streets had vanished with the heat of the summer, leaving only the harsh cold and the empty streets of a January day. Three months had passed since that October, and a month since that letter. The New Year had also started, and with it a feeling of freshness that gradually dispelled the disappointment of not being able to reach the Supreme Court. On the other hand, Fridays of Glory strengthened us, they had grown to the point where crowds could not fit, so we decided to hold another event on a different night of the week.

—*Everything that has happened in these four months is impressive,"* —Sarrail, the owner of the station, told me. —*However, I am worried about one thing: there are many who have come, many who have been saved, but walk like sheep that have no shepherd. Dionny, what are you going to do with all these people? They see you as a guide,*

209

who knows if maybe God has you in this city for this reason.

— It could be, — I said—. But I am still not sure what God wants with us, because I know there's something I should do in Miami, but at the same time; I also know that we are not finished here.

The month of February arrived and Yari and I continued the fast that we had begun since October, even though we had not achieved what we wanted in terms of our legal battle, our perspective had changed. We no longer fasted to see a result in our favor, we fasted for all the things that were already in our favor. That February God dealt deeply with our spirit, I felt that we had finally transcended. We began to enjoy an unexplained inner peace totally alienated from places, circumstances, or what others thought.

The month of March came and I remember finding myself on the phone with Ferney Paez, from Bogota Colombia, son of apostle Gustavo. They are great friends who were there for us during a great deal of our process. Apostle Gustavo runs the Oasis Federation of Churches and his son oversees the whole youth ministry.

— I know you cannot travel, but we need you here at our camp in June of this year. I feel that

something is going to burst —Ferney added, with his peculiar manner of speaking, and continued —*I will do all the publicity announcing that you are coming. I am going to do it as an act of faith.*

— *Do not do that* — I said, laughing. — *We cannot let people down.*

—*We are not going to let them down. We have been praying a lot and I feel something. You will remember me.*

Without success in making him change his mind, we agreed. He began an advertising campaign through the media announcing my visit to Colombia. The days went by and I forgot.

—*I still cannot believe it*— I heard Yari say, as she asked me to finish buttoning her dress. Gently with my right hand I managed to remove her light brown curly hair from the back of her neck, discovering the three buttons she could not reach. I could only pause to admire her; her olive skin, her grace, her ferocity, her white dress that gave a celestial touch at that moment. Once again, I realized that I had more reasons to be grateful. Finally, I thought something that surprised me: "Until now perhaps things have not gone exactly as we wanted, but I would not change a single thing, if I could".

After she turned her gaze from the mirror I realized that it was taking too long to get close to helping her. And there we were, in front of the mirror, I also dressed in white.

—I cannot believe it either— I said, smiling. We had unexpectedly accepted the challenge. That Sunday, March the twenty-seventh, we would become the official pastors of "House of Glory"

When I got to the place I remember seeing all of them dressed in white, it was like a big wedding where we made a vow with God to manifest his purpose for Philadelphia, whatever it was. We surrendered our dreams and personal goals to His, instantly any residue of anxiety, fear or disappointment that existed in me, disappeared altogether.

From revelation to manifestation

"The steps of a good man are ordered by the Lord, and He delights in his way".

(Salmos 37:23).

Time seemed to have passed too quickly. Definitely the decision to shepherd was unexpected, but more

212

unexpected was the call we would receive a few days later.

— *Dionny, are you ready for this?* — It was Jamie, our lawyer. I had not heard his voice for months.

—*And now what?* — I asked, a little nervous, as if expecting to hear something bad.

—*From what I've seen you've been praying a lot* — he added jokingly. — *I received a call from the Court, they want to reassess your case, Judge Harold has been in the middle of a scandal and retired. The prosecutor has been fired. There is a new Judge named Brown and wants you to appear on May 9 of this year.*

—*But that's in a month's time!*

—*Sure.*

You can imagine my reaction, I did not know whether to laugh or to cry, whether to be happy or worried.

—*There's nothing to worry about, Dionny, nothing bad can come out of this, they cannot give you a worse sentence, they just want to reevaluate.*

We spent some time on the phone, talking about what this would mean, and even about the possibility that the sentence would be postponed.

Deferred ... would it be possible?
The day arrived. It was a cool day, clear, blue as the sea. A warm breeze announced that winter had stopped and summer was about to begin.

This time my mother was with us. Between a mixture of nervousness and emotion I opened the doors of the red Jeep Wrangler that I had given my mother years ago. The two entered and finally I did. I will never forget to take 95 south, the highway that led to the Court. I inserted the CD "Holy Crew 2", an urban music album in which "PBC", a singer friend, had asked me to participate, years before everything started. I had written and sang along with Yari on one song, track 7 of the second album, I searched for it, and when I turned the volume up, the song began. Yari and I could not resist the temptation to sing it from that car with a loud voice.

I thought I lost, but then I understood.

That by his blood victory I received.

Defeats do not exist God never failed

And that same power now I have it.

And now let us celebrate His freedom.

I have victory, victory.

Because Satan is defeated, I will sing.

I have victory, victory.

Before I fought the battle, I won it.

I have victory, victory.

And everything in the end will work for good.

I have victory, victory.

If there is someone who hears this who thinks he
or she is losing.

You feel that you will not have to win,

because you have tried everything Greater is the one
with us do not fear

From the abyss that you are today, God says you
should get out.

And finally, the rap part came in, while Yari and I
sang to the top of our voices from the car, living the
whole song:

Look how much more, more, you have made
me victorious

You gave me strength like the bear
Your power is so glorious, how beautiful.

You protect my abode as a bailiff.

Who cares if a thousand come against me?

Who cares they want to kill me?

Let them break it they are going to have to pay the

"bill" I kept the receipts

When God gives account to my enemies, all will be inactive

And will see Dionny Baez is with the Almighty...

It is impressive that that song has written without me ever knowing what would happen. We played it again and again, until we got to the parking lot of the Court. Singing it so many times had created a powerful effect, we got out of the car sure that it did not matter what would happen; things were going to be in our favor.

And one last time there we were, in the same cold corridor, before the same majestic red wooden door, about to enter the same room number 1103 of the same Court. But something had changed ... we were not the same. The cold, the door, and the atmosphere no longer frightened us.

We entered with total peace disconnected from the outcome of that day. A conviction that was difficult to explain.

Our lawyer had already met for a few minutes with the new judge and the new prosecutor behind closed doors. Apparently, they had briefly touched upon the decisive points to be discussed this day, then they went out through that little door beside the pedestal, the same one that the Judge used to enter and leave the room. My lawyer looked at me and smiled as he quickly closed his eyes, as if he wanted to send me a message. He began the same routine until the moment could not wait any longer.

— *Dionny Baez vs. Commonwealth of Pennsylvania.*

— *Your Honor* — my lawyer began. —*As you have seen, the evidence presented above does not carry the weight to keep my client as charged. Therefore, today I ask the verdict against him to be abolished.*

As the judge glanced at the papers, she looked up at the new prosecutor and asked, —Do you have any objections?

—*No, your honor*— she answered without hesitation.

The supervising officer was standing on the left side of the prosecutor.

—*You?* —the judge asked.

— *No, your honor.*

And so simply, so easily, so fast, what we had asked for so much, for what we had fought for years, our greatest request was answered. God had to exhibit and eliminate the past system to give us the present victory.

Trying to put into words what I felt at that moment is futile, but I can instead describe what happened. Yarissette squeezed my hand so tightly that I thought she was going to break it, as she made small noises as if she was screaming inside. I could not contain the joy. On the other hand, my mother could not control herself and began to cry. I slowly put my hand on her back. As for me, what can I say? As for me ... I can only say that I smiled, I smiled so hard.

The Judge had not dictated her conclusion yet, but we all knew what was coming.

—*Without any objection, the verdict issued has been lifted.*

How sweet was the sound of the hammer, tack-tack! wood against wood, announcing absolute freedom.

Jamie approached the judge while she signed some papers, the prosecutor packed some folders in her briefcase and the supervisor just got up and left.

—Congratulations, Dionny, —said Jamie, smiling after receiving a piece of paper from the judge. He tapped my shoulder inviting me to go out of the room. We all left in a hurry.

— *You're a free man, I'm very happy for you.*

The truth is, we did not pay much attention to Jamie's words, we just hugged and laughed. At last I shook Jamie's hand and gave him a hug.

— *And now what?* —I asked.

—*Nothing can bother you now. Oh, and you can travel anytime you want. Although I would give it a couple of days so the system can be updated*
— Added Jamie, handing me the decree.

What a happy day. The first thing that occurred to us was to go to have breakfast and celebrate somewhere.

Life is in the details

"If you pay close attention, if you look beyond the distractions you will find God in every detail."

—*I told you so* —Ferney repeated over and over again, after finding out about

HOW TO WIN YOUR WORST

what had happened. In fact, in early June I was in Colombia, my first trip after a long time. The event was glorious, and I celebrated with the crowd the blessing of being there. But there were other surprises waiting for me.

After returning to Philadelphia, I decided to paint and fix our church building.

— *But what color do I paint it?* — I asked myself that morning. It was still June and I knew I had to take advantage of the summer for the relevant upgrades in the building.

—Blue maybe? It represents heaven, a sacred place.

While I was asking me that question, I heard a voice inside of me saying: "It will not be blue".

—*Why, Lord?"* —I answered, and immediately it spoke again, "Because it is not the color that the prophet told you".

—*What prophet?* —I asked.

Immediately I remembered what Paul Lay, the prophet of Patagonia, had prophesied years before: "You will lead a church, you will begin in the month of March, it will be very powerful, crowds will come from many places thirsty for a spiritual incentive, I see the color of the building".

I remembered that showing me a briefcase on the seat he told me: *"The color is like this"*. *Referring to mustard beige...*

"Beige? But this cannot be the church, he told me that it would begin ... in ... the month of ... March! Wow! "Until that moment I had not realized that I had indeed begun on March 27 as the prophet predicted; only two years earlier, he never really said what year it would be.

"But it cannot be, he mentioned some palm trees, different palm trees, before arriving ..."

I was astonished to recall one of my continuous complaints: "Why did they choose those horrible palm trees?", referring to the pile of metallic gray palm trees that a politician ordered to install by fifth street, a short distance before the church. Who knew these palm trees were there for us? That God had used the occurrence of an unknown politician to confirm His word. Impressive, the prophecy was fulfilled to the letter.

The church continued to grow, within a few months we realized that we needed a bigger place. For a long time, I had heard of Felton from Philadelphia, a prestigious "super club" where they held concerts with the most outstanding artists of the moment. Because of an unleashed shooting at the front of the building during one of the concerts, the mayor condemned the place closing it and declaring that alcohol would never again be sold in that place, the license would be suspended without renewal. For three years it had been closed.

Who could be the owner? Will they sell it? But even if they sell it, how could I buy it? The church had only existed for one year and a few months, there was no bank that dared finance us and we definitely did not have the money. However, I dared to contact the owner, who kindly agreed to travel from New York to Philadelphia that same week.

—*"Not to worry, I'll finance it for you myself,"* said Ricardo Lopez, the former owner of Philadelphia's Felton. The price ... three times less than its value. We celebrated our second year as a church in our own building, a strategic move since everyone in the city knew that place. From there, even bigger things began to happen.

Returning to the words of that strange revelation in my room where that character said to me: "in October a hundred times more", this October we decided to begin an unprecedented revival in our city. Surprisingly, "God TV", a worldwide television network with an audience of 900 million viewers, offered to televise live (completely for free) every night of this supernatural event.

Reinhard Bonnke, John Kilpatrick, Israel Houghton and others, have been with us during these impressive nights, where people from all over the world have come and waited in line from three in the afternoon to enter the place at seven o'clock at night.

Today is November the eighteenth of two thousand fourteen, while they are driving me to the revival, I find myself writing the last words of this book in the back seat of my car. Today for twenty-five consecutive days we have been under the glory of God, so many kinds of illnesses have been healed, innumerable people have been transformed, and some nine hundred million people have been connected every night from all parts of the world. world through God TV. What is happening is surprising, I would have never dreamed of such magnitude. Tomorrow we will continue. And the night after tomorrow. And the night after that. I do not know until when, or how far we will go, but one thing I know: each episode took us up to this point. Today I see how all past enemies have been defeated and what was once atrocious, today is a beautiful testimony. I made mistakes and I got things right, I learned so many things. I do not pretend to have achieved everything, I know that other battles will come, but if I have something to treasure it will be this reality: "he who perseveres will realize that his worst battle is only the embryo of his greatest victory; it only needs time".

In the meantime:

1. Have Balance. Remember that without storms there is no peace, and that shadows are only the result of light beyond the obstacle.

2. Apply Resistance. If you want to stop the fight; die to your emotions and keep quiet. Because nobody fights against a dead person.

3. Re-condition. Change your perception, because he who does not act from the spirit, will react from the flesh.

4. Achieve clarity. Remember that lack of forgiveness will only cloud your senses.

5. Handle cause and effect. Keep in mind that in order for the battle to be a miracle, the cause must be love.

6. Execute transformation. Truth and reality are not the same. Your reality may be limited, but the truth is that you are more than you think you are, so be transformed into it and take control of your reality.

7. Synchronize with God. And you will realize that what you call coincidences is nothing more than the miraculous arrangement of events that will define your destiny.

8. Transcend. At this level, you will understand that the material realm is only an illusion and that you do not exist in time and space, therefore you should not be a prisoner of it.

9. And finally express yourself. This will be the time to celebrate your victory and realize that all things work together for good to those who love God, that just every step of the way is ordained by God and that your victory has been coldly calculated.

Have peace, you are going to win your worst battle.

As for Miami, I do not know. Maybe this book is not over yet...

Visit us today and find out about all the author's books.

www.DionnyBaez.com

Man Vs. Glory

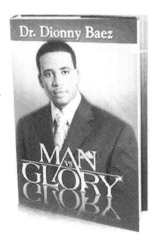